I0711186

New Albion:

The Atlantic Charter and The Arboreal Kingdom

Tom Kawczynski

Copyright © 2020 by Tom Kawczynski

All rights reserved. This book or any portion thereof may not be reproduced or used in any manner whatsoever without the express written permission of the author except for the use of brief quotations in a book review.

Printed in the United States of America

First Printing, 2020

Table of Contents

Introduction

Welcome to the second chapter in the New Albion series laying out the foundations for the Atlantic Homeland. Our precursor motivations are expressed much more fully in *New Albion: The Atlantic Homeland*, now envisioned as the first chapter in what will be a four-volume set to further develop these concepts.

The first book asked why we need to do something radically different to see Western Civilization, American Liberty, and European Culture survive and offered a mental basis for the challenging task ahead. These next three books are designed to offer a first glimpse into how we might accomplish these goals, both in terms of the structures and policies required, and in how we can ethically transition from our current system to our liberation. I ask that you suspend your disbelief long enough to consider what option would be better, and then follow your conscience. Assuming you accept the why, it's time for us to figure out how, which is more complicated but also more rewarding because it gives us a reason for action which adds purpose to life and also hope to our ongoing efforts.

Even though New Albion is perhaps more concerned with culture and lifestyle than governance, this second volume deliberately addresses questions of law, liberty, government, and how we want to structure the state to serve in defense of the nation. Many years in politics have taught me that there are certain people who very much need to see the rules up front to understand the system, and these being the questions which are most often asked about New Albion, I have endeavored my very best herein to offer solutions for many different problems. It is impossible to prepare for every unforeseen situation, to address every particular issue in just twelve mere chapters, and to satisfy everyone. I take it as a matter of necessity that as this project advances, the plan will improve and evolve based upon the contributions of men and women of talent and character who through shrewd reason and observation of nature plug the holes in this skeletal outline being laid out to follow.

Subsequent works imagine an in-depth discussion of the cultural and educational system in the third volume, and considerations upon the economy, environment, and lifestyle in the fourth volume. Less obvious in this volume, but a recurring and deliberate theme you will notice is that New Albion approaches these questions from more of a qualitative perspective as a quantitative approach. A core assertion of our nation from the inception has been we want to choose better over more if forced to decide as a central pivot about for which we desire separation. What this means is when ideas are presented, the arguments that will emerge will not merely be about GDP, statistics, and a host of facts designed to pummel you into submission, but instead a genuine concern about how we build a better world for people by seeking to make ourselves into the better people we want to be. Inherently, there are many tradeoffs about such logic as this represents a sea change in thought from how politics is conducted where we presently argue the virtues of the system and fit people to their requirements. We seek the virtues of our people, and to assemble a system to protect, sustain, and encourage such growth.

With respect to the laws this volume contemplates today, the same pattern holds very much true as the goal here is to create better families, a more rewarding existence for men and women by building a society that reflects and honors the nature of each. This society has latitude for exceptions as we have come to expect from liberty, yet clearly indicates a preferred and broad path that recognizes a society has to defend its majority and sustain that just as clearly as it seeks to protect the minority from unjust persecution. This balance has always been and will always be a struggle, and New Albion deliberately shifts more toward order by presenting responsibility as a core concern to be held in practice and in law as an equal balance to liberty, which many feel has descended into licentiousness and the unending means by which we are restrained from resolving problems a growing majority would like to see addressed.

As you read through the framework espoused, I want to share my personal reflection that in creating this system many alternate models were considered and much historical research was done. There is no perfect system, and every system is fundamentally more contingent upon the integrity of the people and the unity of the culture they create than some magical value we ascribe to laws to hold men together. The Constitution of the United States is brilliant, but it is failing against the decay of our people. No simpler code of laws has ever been imagined than the Ten Commandments, and even that has proven too onerous in this age, so we must start by admitting the limitations inherent to the law. When well designed, laws exist as does the state, primarily to restrain the worst impulses we have, and as such, have an incredibly poor track record when trying to fix people. This is the path of blood and compulsion, and as much as can be reasonably attempted while not making the state unworkable, I've deliberately tried to avoid going down those roads.

In thinking through this model, I have sought to understand the majority of people who make up this land of New Albion, those of pan-European origins, while being mindful of minorities and natives who were here and who have legitimate claims. Our borders always reflect this awareness, but we also accept and admit there are those who will choose to be part of our culture and we want to welcome those who followed us honestly and faithfully as we begin this project anew. Some find that statement insufficient because they believe people cannot co-exist, others because it is too exclusive. Absolute homogeneity has the virtue of greater comfort and unity, but has often slipped into insular indifference that leads to external invasion and lack of innovation. Absolute heterogeneity is even worse, where everything gets reduced to an unhappy least common denominator where few are happy, and no one can speak out lest they give offense. New Albion deliberately marches toward the homogeneous in culture, ethnography, and philosophy, but with mindfulness that we want to challenge ourselves, and that we want to preserve those elements of liberty which have served us well while discarding those which show comparatively little value.

It is important to mention this because this is very much a third way solution where we are putting people before systems, and as such, we can blend ideas from different ideological schools and different structural backgrounds than have ever been done before. The answer that works for our needs is the right answer, and understanding who we are in light of both where we came from and who we desire to be is essential to developing the healthy state and the laws which will protect us from ourselves, by which I mean these descents into absolutism and universalism that cause conflict between states as well as permit the corruption of our societies. The reality is for all the terrors of war, states have committed ten times as much violence against their own people as they have against one another, and in an age where political conflict is the very cause for such unease and agitation, New

Albion wants to escape that cycle and return to something far more natural and sustainable.

The system I propose will have elements which are very familiar, some which have not been used in centuries, and others which are completely novel. I categorically reject the idea that because America was a republic that our solution must come in a republican format. The Founders of our nation emerged from a monarchy and chose the form of governance they thought best suited to the challenges of their day, with several hundred years of success giving credence to their ingenuity. In the same vein, we must be unafraid to consider solutions beyond what we have now, recognizing that the tyranny which will soon be imposed upon us, that of a democratic majority acting in ignorance by a culture which sadly venerates its own anger and stupidity, is the existential threat with which we must contend and which New Albion must restrain and escape if our very civilization is to endure.

The Founders specifically and Enlightenment thinking in general were obsessed with separation between powers as a structural concern and the division between legislative, executive, and judicial authority will be well familiar to most of you. Yet, have we not found in these intervening years that the divisions between who writes the laws, who enforces the laws, and who interprets the laws have become muddied both in practice as well as in the ultimately more important process of how these offices are assigned? I would argue the more salient failure of the American and Canadian systems is the corrosive role of money in appropriating government toward goals which do not serve the broader interests of the nation, the people as a whole, but either narrow ideologies or cynical profiteering on all sides of the spectrum, which is how republics have historically usually fallen. Near the end, as in Rome, they become more democratic using pluralism as a justification, but they descend into a Hobbesian war of all against all whereby everyone screams and no one is heard, a metaphor which perhaps better describes the state of America in 2020 than we would wish.

The question of how we restrain cultural and economic actors from controlling and subverting New Albion has been foremost on my mind, and future volumes will go into exhaustive depth of topics which will only be foreshadowed herein. How money works has to change. How people come to office and are held to account must also. Finding cultural norms that genuinely and organically unite us is the very glue of civilization, yet our media and education in service to oligarchs who promote other interests, teach us precisely the opposite and get wealthy in that enterprise. My anger at such perfidy is palpable, enough so that I am forging a new nation to remove such injustice, but I mention these things here because we need to be mindful that while there is no perfect system, the real problems we face in a culture war that is deeper and crueler than mere political conflict must be resolved lest a new state just be a pretty trapping incapable of birthing a new and healthy nation.

The American and Canadian experiences have revealed that while there is something to be said for separation of how power is exercised, that having horizontal integration as we basically see at the federal level serves as a siphon to draw power and resources away from the people. Ample evidence exists in the great wealth of the cosmopolitan centers most resplendent in the well-heeled national capitals, especially in comparison to the relative poverty and struggles elsewhere throughout the periphery. A less generous person would correctly identify this as theft, not just of the people resources, but of their very spirit, vitality, and morality, because we are being crafted into servants instead of citizens, and whether we serve the whims of the ultra-wealthy or the dictates of some artificial system, we still have abandoned our foundational desire for which our ancestors braved journeys to these shores, to have a different life and a better one in self-determination. To do that, people need access to power and meaningful ability to resist and restrain the state.

In an America worth trillions of dollars, one voter, one family, or one community cannot hope to accomplish such an outcome, and we know it. For as rabidly as maybe half the people fight one another over policy in two contesting camps, the other half of our people have surrendered the fight recognizing this as just an indelible corruption from which they only hope not to face undue bother as they seek to live their lives. If you really think about it, it's tragic that so many people feel only disconnected or agitated, and these numbers are out there to be read to see how pissed off we all have become. Yet, we remain so trapped in dialectical reasoning, us versus them, at the partisan, structural, and national levels, that we have thus far ignored none of the options before us in that framework seem likely to see us in a happier place.

New Albion believes our greatest asset is our human capital, the limitless potential of our people, and we act upon it in this framework not as a rhetorical point to win a vote, but as the fundamental division upon which our system is based as we seek deliberately to return power to you every time we can and everywhere it makes sense. We understand that the separation of powers which our time requires is vertical between four levels of community, county, principality (state/province), and kingdom (crown). At local levels, where people can be held to account, such as the community and county, you have elections, civic engagement, and elections beyond partisanship. At higher levels, New Albion elevates those of talent to serve as a dedicated civil service, culminating in an elected monarch who exists to unite culture, defend the realm, and promote development. Money is divided between the levels. How people come to office is also divided. And yet, cooperation is required, because New Albion recognizes different roles require different personalities.

A nation requires a strong singular leader to articulate a vision that unites the people. We cannot keep changing what we believe wholesale every few years and hope for anything but conflict and stagnation. Such a leader should be constrained to serve in the interests and defense of the people, as clearly and deliberately developed in a strengthened Bill of Rights and Responsibilities, but the King must also recognize his job is to inspire and mobilize the nation and serve to watch the public interest as his own. A few big things that matter to us all, and helping with the smaller things has been the hallmark of excellence in leadership, and New Albion demands that of our monarch and the higher civil service.

But we know that we are different people. Quebec is not Maine, and Nova Scotia is not Vermont. Furthermore, Montreal is not Augusta, and Halifax is not Rutland. We want the power to decide most things to remain local. To the individual, to the family, to the community, and to the county in that precise order. Work collaboratively, transcend ideology, find consensus in the community, and have the county serve as your legislator, your judge, and execute most tasks so that we all live how our lands require and the lifestyles we desire. City and country folk are different, but the idea we're forced to adhere to the same laws and restrictions is leading us to fight. Let's try a different way and separate out powers and authorities where everyone can survive, can learn from one another, and we root all we do in those closest to us, not someone ruling imperiously from afar.

It is not hard to imagine a better system. In practice, I've found every time I spend at least an hour with people who think on these questions, regardless of their origin, background, or ideology, we can all do so much better than what we presently accept, we can solve some and address so many more relevant issues than these countries which hold us even try to answer. Because they're owned and occupied, which is something I hope you understand intuitively at this point, and for which I invite you to read any of my books on America for a painful description of how our land was conquered by cynicism and deceit. But in such a situation, where our culture is weaponized against us, we face daily and constant psychological, moral, and spiritual intimidation and degradation against our interests always speaking against hope and renewal.

There was good reason why I dedicated my entire first book not just to explaining why New Albion is necessary, but also in trying to kindle a fire in the reader to believe that action is not just essential but that we also can still make a difference. It is easy to lose hope these days, but the most rewarding part of this project has been seeing people come back to live and recognize that while America may be prostrate and Canada under submission, that our people endure, and we may yet renew ourselves.

With such inspiration, let us think together how we can live better, and allow this humble suggestion to serve as framework which does not end the discussion, but begins asking those

questions we have too long ignored and pushes public the
question of what we do now with this offering of New Albion.

Chapter One: Basic Principles

As this book will be highly technical at times and concerned with much detail and argument about why specific measures are being arranged in the precise manner chosen, it seemed important to use the first chapter to outline the key underlying principles employed in all these suggestions which follow.

The first obvious requirements are that we want to uphold our core values of reason, nature, grace, and loyalty, recognizing our goal to put people before systems, and to seek that which is better over that which is easier. Consider those the essential impetus of all we do in New Albion in service of resurrecting Western Civilization, which we believe to be inextricable from the people of European origin who birthed such and the cultural ideals which service us now as they have for millennia. In addition to that, we considered deeply the experiences of our first few centuries on this new continent we are still learning and settling, and what American liberty and Canadian loyalty have to teach.

The second thing we want to work toward is recognizing that we need to vertically disassemble the existing state to regain our liberty, identity, and sovereignty, undo the control mechanisms that bind us, and create an alternative that is faithful to the original settlers vision of living the good life in a new land. What this means is we return power as locally as we can, and that starts with the individual and the family, two institutions we venerate and protect, but recognizing clearly while rights are individual, families are the basic smallest self-sustaining unit of any society. In New Albion, no man ever has to be an island.

Having laid out those broad trajectories, there are five basic criteria by which we consider all that we create, and I will discuss these here rather than interrupting every future discussion to demonstrate the values at work. As this narrative develops, my goal will be much more to demonstrate how the ideas work in the real world, but as policy should not be divorced from principle if we hope to build a ethnical society in our new nation, it seems important to have this discussion as preliminary to all else.

In no way reflective of their respective importance, the five key factors employed in the creation of the law and governance for New Albion can be symbolized by the acronym **FLASH**. Flexible, local, accountable, simple, and honest is what we want our laws to be, how we demand our government works, and why we believe everyone can understand and benefit from our system.

Let's start with flexibility. How many people hate lawyers? Odds are pretty good you said yes unless you happen to be employed in the legal profession, and we find so often that debates and procedure get caught up in arcane deliberation which is incomprehensible to all but those most deeply involved. How often have we seen guilty people go free on a technicality, or a good man trapped in the system due to some law that forces compliance? Too often in my opinion, and this happens because we have placed undue majesty upon the law as a stricture that binds us.

We also see this same mindset manifest in our politics. We are continually reminded and constantly forced to do things in ways that are far less efficient or useful than we might because the system requires we adhere to its rules. Whether it is in service to a corrupt bureaucracy, or being trapped where votes mean nothing because laws pushed by judges who exist beyond any account undo the popular will, we live in an ossified system where the vitality of the people is actively suppressed by the rigidity of the process.

New Albion breaks these bounds by being **flexible** as a core value. In our nation, there is not a law to govern every single act between two people because we believe that we have the maturity to exist as actors with agency. We trust our people to act responsibly within a few clearly delineated laws which will be laid out in the next four chapters to cover rights, responsibilities, criminal and civil law. We also expect and desire that different counties will choose different paths as befit their customs, and as American states and Canadian provinces originally did, we welcome this variety as an opportunity to experiment toward finding better solutions and recognize that life in the hills is different than along the coast, in the prairies, or near the lakes.

Flexibility is what America once had and what it gave up during the last hundred years as we came to value systems more than people. Losing that latitude is what has us on the brink of yet another brothers' war, this time a civil war to destroy the last vestiges of liberty still extant in the West, all in service of an elite who use their money and status to manipulate us thusly. We win when we fight them, not each other, and for all but those who want to force compulsion for whom we offer separation as final settlement, we can find ways to accommodate under the New Albion banner all those of good will who share our dream.

Without saying, it is obvious such a system must be highly **local**. As described briefly above, the American experiment has proven that our people when permitted to exist in our own self-interest can achieve accomplishments unseen in the world before when we serve our own families, communities, and country. As

Tocqueville shrewdly observed, our goodness has ever been the source of our greatness, not the magnitude of our government or the extent of our foreign commitments. It is not independence that made America succeed, but interdependence which are organic bonds that exist between people, voluntarily renewed, and forged with intent in pursuit of common and greater purpose.

We start with individual rights, and the Atlantic Charter which will be laid out in full detail in the next two chapters offers the strongest protection of individual rights anywhere in the world, incorporating the genius of Patrick Henry and strengthening those resolutions into something even firmer for our day and age with new protections added for both individuals and families alike against the many encroachments of the state as well as the compulsions of an alien culture which seeks to restrain our vitality.

I believe firmly in order, hierarchy, and purpose, recognizing restraint is what makes civilization possible, and acknowledging that the West has been built upon such values. But such thought only has meaning for free men who choose deliberatively, are permitted to develop their fullest potential. Therefore, we must enshrine those liberties ever more firmly into law should we desire not to have a petty despotism buy off the demise for one generation, but instead forge the foundation for renewal.

We build upwards from there, defending the family, and in accordance with our understanding of nature, seeing men and women as different, vital, essential, and complementary partners in the inescapable duty of raising families in love and comfort. Life is the purpose, love is the means, but to protect these things, we must always remember the family needs our support. Instead of trying to break it apart to seize control as those who occupy the height of culture and government now attempt, we return power to husbands and wives, mothers and fathers, and to men and women to protect and raise their children as they see fit, and to no longer have the state serve so frequently as intermediary and interlocutor to tear this social fabric apart.

The same principles apply as we advance through the ranks of power in how the government itself is structured. People have greater say, greater flexibility, and greater choice locally and get involved as we want local participation. You're setting up your future, and New Albion wants you to be inspired. Town meetings mean every budget needs your approval, and every year, you select a new mayor who will be held to account for not just the town, but the legislature they give us.

Some would find it ironic to have a presumptive monarchy choose localism as a virtue, but the biggest job of the King which I try my best to undertake as Regent in this transition is to help our people recover themselves, to revitalize our communities, and to see the spirit of our folk re-emerge. We focus so often on what happens outside our borders and not nearly enough on how we remember what we could be within those, and my focus as this whole project shares is to help you remember.

I can write about a fairy tale. But only you can make it real.

How do we get there? Let's build upon the third value and be **accountable** in all that we do. So many of the problems we experience in America and Canada are because our politicians lie to us and we simply accept this as the cost of doing business. Sometimes, we accept this because we prefer to hear the lies versus facing more challenging truths, and this cowardice is anathema to a New Albioner (pronounced New All-Be-Honor) who recognizes that we must deal with reality as it exists. We demand more of ourselves. As we do so, we also must hold our public servants to that same standard, which is a duty the public has shirked for entirely too long, and which the confrontational nature of our republics becoming democracies happily overlooks.

I understand how strategic voting works and that we have all too often been forced into cynical defense of the lesser of two evils for fear of a quicker degradation. Frankly, that is essentially the mission statement of both the Conservative and Republican Parties: Select us because we won't make things worse. As events have demonstrated and continue quite clearly to reveal, that is not nearly good enough if we are to survive, let alone thrive as we would be right to expect and demand. We need to transform our mindset to expect our government to work well, our laws to protect us, and to hold to account all those acts of malfeasance against us which do not just degrade the wronged parties, but undermine the very confidence and trust upon which liberty itself requires.

In an age of identity politics, I would be remiss if to not apply the question of accountability to this as well. For too many years, many different groups have claimed victim status upon supposed historical incidents, of greater or lesser validity, and have wielded guilt like a weapon to compel submission by well-intentioned people in our society to surrender our reason and serve their ends. With New Albion, this ends. For those who cannot accept this, our eventual separation plan envisions states for those who either want to live as perpetual victims in the coastal enclaves beyond current repair, or for those who come from non-European backgrounds who genuinely assert a desire to build a nation in accordance with their cultural impulses, a separation into lands where they can be sovereign is a conversation we welcome on peaceful terms. All grievances will be settled, no reparations will be paid, but separation on principled and peaceful disintegration is how we announce we are taking account for ourselves and for a new future born neither in supremacy nor inferiority, but where the empire we seek to conquer is in finding the best version of ourselves.

New Albion is a movement conceived in love, that has a place for those who are not like us who want to be and who demonstrate such through actions and good intent. Grace reveals honest faith through good works, not through the victim mentality that turns men into weaklings and allows liars to bring us to their level. We must be more truthful than that with others and with ourselves.

If these ideas seem incredibly **simple**, that is no accident either as this nation believes that you should be able to understand every law, every value, and how our government works as long as you have a basic understanding of the world and a command of normal language. So often, fancy words and deliberate complexity are introduced as a trick of verbal sophistry to confuse people into giving away their power to so-called experts. We don't want our people giving up anything, and so everything shared herein is designed to be accessible and approachable.

As anecdote, I once received a critique of my writing that it has been written so that a third grader can understand all that I share with you. The person making this suggestion, having earned several advanced degrees at a prominent university, was incensed at the popularity of these ideals, but as I later explained, it's because the best ideas are those which everyone can understand and apply to their lives. We can all appreciate there are times for ingenuity and intricacy, and it would actually be easier to express

New Albion in arcane and specialized language to satisfy the cosmopolitan patois whose halcyon continuity they so wish to extend. But I would sound like a pompous ass, no one would listen, many would not understand, and I would be killing a movement from the onset just to express my own insecurity and need for self-aggrandizement.

The person in question is not nearly as bad as this would sound, but I share this story because we have an unhealthy habit of giving too much credence to experts based on their degrees or professional stature and too little respect for common sense. Simplicity can often solve a problem in seconds or minutes that takes others hours or days to resolve when complex external criteria are applied.

New Albion likes to keep things simple. We don't make laws about everything because we recognize situations will occur that are exceptional and will have to be dealt with individually. This is why our legal code has a few clear red lines, a lot of latitude for the judges at the county level, and appeal measures in case we get it wrong. Our rights and responsibilities are just as clear, and we firmly believe they must be understood as written.

Through no fault of their own, we have seen the desires of the Founders in the clear Amendments to the United States Constitution tortured into false meanings by activist judges, and so a final aspect of simplicity is to make comprehensible the law which is clearly and deliberately meant to be understood as written in the fullest aspect imaginable with all deference for this and all times to the citizenry in free will and exercise of their rights. These books can be used as corollary and evidence to this statement and should a day come in the future of New Albion where some alternative is posited, you have the blessings and the strongest advice of our Founders to remove those people as far from power as possible through whatever means necessary.

This new nation we imagine is a revolutionary beginning and restoration, and we are **honest** about our intentions, our purpose, and in what we write and why we say these things. So often, we have been forced into silence or submission through various levers of pressure employed against us, and our desire is to see these sorry days quickly end.

One cannot apprehend reason unless one can be honest about what one thinks. One cannot comment intelligently about nature unless one can be honest about one observes. One cannot offer or receive grace unless one can be honest about identifying that which is obviously false. One cannot work in loyal companionship with their fellow countrymen unless one can be honest about their goals and intentions developed as a shared imperative. Without honesty, we die, and we have been marching blindly for too long along that path without questioning why.

The first book went into exhaustive detail on the question, but I wish to exhort once again that we must be willing to face truth and build our society in not just defense but also pursuit of this goal. When we accept the million little lies that make life easier so we get along, the price is that part of ourselves we can no longer express lest we give offense. Done once, it might very well be a kindness and a mercy, but done so frequently as we have now adopted as habit, we live in a world where are we forced to either accept lies or face ostracism.

New Albion is a true and unapologetic kingdom which often gives offense not because we seek to be cruel, but because we think it kinder to share reality and give people the chance to live honestly or find improvement than to lie and tell people what they wish to be true. I know many people would prefer if I wrote yet another paean to the brilliance of the republic, how all people are equal, that everything will work out, and all because we are still great. If it were true, I'd say that. But it's not, and you wouldn't be reading this if you didn't already know that in your heart of hearts, which is why instead, in fidelity to you, both the words in this book and the systems it creates deal with the reality as it is.

Honesty is truly its own reward and the essential component to maintaining and rebuilding the trust upon which all free societies must rely. Our words are plain but self-evident. Our intentions are public and assertive. We are revolutionaries who will take our own nation, not because we want a fight, but because we cannot help but be who we are: A better people always self-improving. I pray it comes in peace, but either way, it must come.

Between these values, it should be easy to see how they mutually reinforce one another, and all the efforts that follow try to reconcile these traits with our primary goals in seeking to better ourselves. New Albion offers honest and simple solutions, devolved to the most logical local level, providing flexibility but demanding accountability. Now that you know where we are coming from, we're ready to look at the first plan which we hope serves as foundation for something truly special: A blueprint for a new beginning.

Chapter Two: Bill of Rights

These next two chapters will delineate the *Atlantic Charter*, which is designed to be our core statement of principle when it comes to the rights we will protect as inviolate and the responsibilities we accept as a sacred duty in New Albion. Before we get into the rights, it is important to acknowledge that these rights unless clearly otherwise indicated accrue strictly to the individual. The extension of citizen rights to corporations has been one of the most pernicious decisions made by the West, and something we oppose vehemently in New Albion because of how these sanctions have been misused which we will cover in a future volume.

In what is a deliberate and recurring pattern, we have chosen to select twelve basic rights to defend as the starting point for what we consider foundational. Our thinking here is heavily influenced by the popular and highly relevant section of the United States Constitution. We have eliminated nothing, expanded upon some, and are adding others to reflect the changing nature of our world and restrain the means we observe the current state having used to gain control over the people and their liberty. These will apply from day one, and New Albion already endorses these in all our programmatic thinking. For ease of comprehension, we've also tried to match up the numbers in a very familiar way.

The question of amendment is one to be settled later, but the initial thinking is the creation of any new right would require a 75% plebiscite and no existing right can be removed from the public. Freedom should not lapse even in the progression of society. Unlike the Constitution which includes the Bill of Rights as Amendments, the Atlantic Charter is a statement of the Rights and Responsibilities only, so governmental changes would happen within code and tradition, hence the differences. These distinctions will become clearer in a future chapter, but let us cover the protected rights which are put here in their simplest form:

I. Free Speech, Assembly, Association, and Worship

Most Americans venerate and celebrate free speech, but we have seen an encroachment against these rights in several different ways in the last century, and New Albion will restore this liberty.

Let us begin with free speech. While we have this as a nominal right, the reality is between controlled media and deliberate censorship on social media platforms, dissident voices have been targeted, attacked, and boycotted. We will undo these slights and see the creation of a public square that exists both online and offline that is content neutral beyond clearly stated obscenity exemptions primarily to protect children because we want free speech back. Social media in New Albion will not be permitted to silence voices using reason to discover truth because of hurt feelings.

Publishers are going to face a different world also, as we are going to push back hard against the propagandizement of our people. Media will be local once more. We will work to disrupt those conglomerates who leverage their wealth to control the message instead embracing a model where the content creators retain control and are permitted free license to shape our society.

Free association is also crucial to New Albion because we believe in the right of exclusion. For several decades, the government has forced people to associate with those whom they would not choose. That requirement seems to negate the very concept of exercising free will in the choice of companions. While our state will service all our citizens as will those entities which use tax dollars, the reality is you should have the right to be as anti-social or selective in your socialization as you so choose so long as you do not violate the criminal boundaries of the law. America has forced us to accept many things again and again the people did not want, and New Albion represents a return to individual choice which we believe will be more satisfying and create greater tranquility.

Assembly and worship are highly interlinked in practice, so let me start by saying that the rights of people in congregations to speak freely have been basically subsumed for nearly a half century now because of IRS regulations in the United States designed deliberately to muzzle pastors at the pulpit, and to silence leaders who make the logical assertion of the connection between politics, culture, and social outcomes. Selective enforcement of these rules against those who preserve tradition has been endemic, and we want to end this compulsion via nonprofit and revenue collection against people speaking truth. All groups may say what they want in New Albion without fear of pecuniary punishment.

Discussion aside, we believe free speech as a value exists to develop our minds and advance our society. There are challenges to being able to say and do what we want that require a higher level of citizenship than most countries have tried or can keep, but we believe our human talent is equal to the task and see this as an inexorable part of our American legacy we will defend.

II. Self-Defense, Arms, and Militia

As we watch the ongoing efforts by the hostile media and deceptive politicians to remove this bedrock assurance of liberty one act a time, New Albion goes the opposite direction and argues for the expansion and clarification of our second amendment to provide for greater security for the populace as individuals and in defense of all other rights.

Our belief is the clear intent of the Founders of the American vision was to provide means for citizens to offer armed resistance against tyranny from their own government as clearly as threats from without, and they believed a well-armed and trained population would be the essential guarantor of liberty. As we see the very political resistance in America now relying upon this argument for survival against their own replacement, we have ample evidence their assertion was correct.

As was originally envisioned, we essentially seek to preserve the rights for individuals to arm themselves alone or collectively to the level of irregular infantry including the expansion of access to light arms that presupposes which would be appropriate for a militia. Furthermore, as part of the New Albion primary education process, children will be instructed upon proper use and care of basic weaponry, with militias to be deliberately maintained at the county level for all who want to participate as a sanctioned enterprise by the state subject to the people within those counties.

You will be able, expected, and encouraged to defend yourself and your home, as we believe not only in the protection that weaponry permits, but that it creates a more civil and respectful society by creating the implied responsibility of civil behavior between people. We expect a low crime rate and high trust because the reality is the capacity for violence makes people think far more carefully about their actions than one where chaos reigns as now.

For those most familiar with the American Bill of Rights, you will note that we have moved quartering, the practice of housing soldiers in the homes of citizens, away from its original spot and though likely obsolete, this protection is retained under the succeeding amendment that greatly strengthens privacy protections. For the new third amendment, we have chosen to adopt a protection that for all citizens, and only for citizens, there is the guarantee of equal protection under law in the application of all these rights and responsibilities.

We have adopted this provision because America has become a place where certain groups have protections and status other people do not, and` we want to destroy this idea of a protected class as antithetical to the unity we desire at the heart of our society. Either everyone, or every group enjoys a protection, or none do. We will not have policies where the government gives advantages in contracting, in educational accession, and employment to one group because of so-called victim status as opposed to other citizens of our country.

To be clear, there are two obvious exceptions which need to be highlighted here, which is that it is entirely appropriate for policy to be created which protects certain special, natural, and innate functions which are involved with children and women. We will protect our children, and recognize the nature of childbearing requires certain protections for women that are biologically necessary and socially desirable, but this amendment is meant to destroy group identity as a lever to be used against the majority.

Such action about meritocracy applies to legal equity, government policy, tax conduct, and entities so affiliated. Importantly, this does not and should not be used to negate the right to free association or free dissociation of private entities. Our belief and hope is that all who engage and conduct commerce in our economy will choose a path of openness in this saner society, but we recognize the right of exclusion and to choose to whom one will provide service, on what basis, and for whatever criteria one so chooses.

We believe the best will win out, and our better nature will shine through with all groups benefitting from being held in equal regard and to a common standard instead of arbitrary distinctions.

IV. Privacy, Against Search and Seizure, Warrants, Quartering

In America, the right to privacy has been utterly shredded and all the terrible acts by our own treasonous Deep State has shown just how essential these protections are. What the Patriot Act undid and what is ignored elsewhere is restored fully and more strongly in New Albion. Not only do we want to enshrine these rights, but consider it a key element of this new government that we want to avoid the very creation of those institutions that have led to such misuse in a compromised judiciary, overwrought bureaucracy, and self-appointed law enforcement apparatus at the Federal level.

With this right, warrants will once again be needed to collect information on potential suspects absent the obvious situation where a crime is being directly observed. Such warrants will not proceed from secret courts and shadowy figures, but will instead come from the county level as was intended.

The government has zero presumptive right to enter your residence without your permission absent your consent or a lawfully obtained warrant. As our government will be deliberately much weaker, we are placing greater trust in our citizens, and we believe this healthier society will reduce tension and increase collegiality.

The prohibition against quartering also remains here, but this applies not just to the stationing of soldiers in your residence, but also to unlawful surveillance by electronic device. In an age of smart devices, we will not permit the government the ability to passively spy upon, intercept, or compel blanket delivery of information for the hopes of randomly turning our people into criminals. The same warrant protections which apply to your person should also apply to your data.

Your liberty is your own and we want to defend it absent compelling evidence having been duly considered in a court of law to act against you on any grounds of suspicion. The days where we treat our own citizens as criminals must come to a permanent end.

V. Against Self-Incrimination

The basic right against self-incrimination has been one of the better parts of the American legal system, and we have chosen to maintain that right as part of an effective defense. The presumed obligation remains upon the state to have the burden of proof to convict the suspect rather than adopting the presumption of guilt to be disproven as is the case in the Roman legal tradition.

However, while we maintain that right, it is worth noting that the very simplicity and integrity of New Albion law does much to remove the sort of procedural defenses so often used to get guilty people off on technicalities. Our laws are deliberately designed to be understood by all, will be taught by all, and the days where someone could claim ignorance of the law to escape prosecution or punishment will be removed. Chapter Four covers the twelve major offenses, and for those issues that exist in the inevitable gray areas, we deliberately leave latitude to the locally elected judges and juries by peer.

VI. Require Human Accuser

Given how invasive technology has become and all the ways in which it could be possibly misused, New Albion feels it is important enough to assert this right that we deliberately made it a Charter requirement that any case being brought against a person have a human accuser as opposed to mere technological evidence, or should this evolve, some form of artificial intelligence. Data or pattern recognition absent human corroboration is not enough.

One of the evolving trends of how intelligence is gathered and people's behavior is being predicted is the use of various artificial means to extrapolate likely actions and responsibility, and while these tools will certainly open doors that will be useful for some areas, we reject going down the path of allowing machines to make decisions for our people. Ultimately, we adopt human sovereignty as a core element of New Albion and this right is the bedrock that ensures the protection of our people from the evolution of technology in service of the state.

While we cannot fully imagine the evolution of what this amendment may come to encapsulate, our intention here is to ensure that our society remains for humans and by humans, a question which we think may prove to be of some import and the not so distant future, and to which we can only offer the guidance that we should be very careful what other forms of intelligence we even consider as potential competitors in our future society.

VII. Criminal Trial by Jury, Appeal, Civil Claims by Judge, Speedy Trial

All issues related to the justice system are condensed into this single amendment designed to greatly simplify our legal process and to speed up the execution of justice as well as protect the citizens against long periods of incarceration.

For criminal trials, the system grants the unique opportunity to resolve these claims by a jury of their peers, or to have the judge, who will be the Count as selected by the elected. It is no accident that the people who make the laws also enforce and adjudicate the laws in New Albion as we wanted our leaders to be directly connected to their policy and the people so impacted.

The right of appeal in any decision is guaranteed where a court may be assembled of three mayors randomly chosen from within the country of jurisdiction no less than once per month to consider such cases, either for sentencing alone or the adjudication itself.

Civil trials do not have the right to a jury, but instead will be settled equitably by the judge, which is the Count and his staff of arbiters. This will greatly accelerate and simplify the legal process.

All trials must be begun within thirty days of the charging of a person or filing of a claim, and must be complete within sixty days at which point a verdict will be rendered. Appeals must be complete with a thirty-day window for criminal trials.

The amount of time, money, and energy we invest into our legal system for years has been utterly obnoxious, and these provisions are designed to make this system work much more quickly, which reflects a far simpler legal code appropriate to New Albion.

VIII: Parental Sovereignty, Family Integrity

For many years, we've seen the ongoing encroachment of child protective services into the family, and this trend has resulted in all sorts of bizarre cases that have essentially resulted in state sanctioned kidnapping of children. This amendment puts an end to that practice, forbidding the creation of state confiscatory agencies of children and removing that temptation and function. Your children are your own to raise as you see fit absent clear signs of physical abuse, trauma, or malnourishment. In those cases, such issues will be settled before a local court as a matter of criminal action as assault against a minor.

These extreme cases are mentioned only as a reminder that criminal law still applies here to the protection of all people, including minors, but what this means is the choice of education, lifestyle, upbringing, and the decision to employ traditional corporal punishment will be preserved. Our goal is not to endorse any particular method of parenting, but rather to restrain ourselves from intervening in the rights of a family.

Absent tangible evidence of abuse, this amendment also conveys equal parental rights including custody to the mother and father of a child. Both will be assumed equally responsible for any child, regardless of their marital status, and our legal system will remove itself from playing intermediary in legal cases related to questions of alimony and child support as matters reserved to the family and toward which we have no inclination to overstep our authority.

For too long, the government has tried to replace and manage families. The people must act more responsibly and learn how to voluntarily do this themselves, so we will absent ourselves in faith that without our intervention these issues may be resolved through mutual understanding and the concern natural for progeny.

IX: Bodily Sovereignty, Health Choice

In New Albion, your body is considered sacrosanct. The state has no presumed right to require any treatment, injection, augmentation, or other deviation of any kind upon you without your freely given consent. For too long, we have seen medical warrants used as a means of control, and to respect the integrity of your body and mind, our medical practice will be restricted from offering any material adjustment to you absent your consent.

In these last few years, we've watched the encroachment of mental health into areas of life that were once unthinkable where people have been subject to treatments as if they had a disability for behaviors that were once considered normal and natural, like masculinity and femininity. By putting the veneer of medicine over top of social programming, the state has found a new avenue to try to convert people against their will to conformity, and we believe these actions are not commensurate with liberty and free thought.

As such, we are proactively writing into law protections from the medical overreach, but also against any idea that you might later be compelled to augment your body through the introduction of mechanical apparatuses to enhance your capacities. We want you to find your fullest expression of self as a complete human being, and this law is designed to protect your corpus. The right applies to all bodies, conveying as necessary corollary the right to life as absolute for all human beings who fit this criterion absent voluntary consent publicly given to surrender such.

In addition, we want to ensure health choices are always maintained by the individual or by their freely chosen designee, so the age of forced treatments will hereby end.

X: School Choice

As proud as we are of the education system we are designing which we expect to be preferred by the vast majority of our citizens, and which will be heavily featured in the third book, we would be remiss to our duties in protecting the family if we did not ultimately reserve the right to parents to educate their children as they so desire, allowing for the options of private school, charter schooling, or home schooling as viable alternatives, with any money for education being attached to the student rather than it is now with the publicly held institution.

In New Albion, we balance rights with responsibilities, so please understand any student wishing to assert full citizenship will be required to demonstrate basic competency in reading, writing, and arithmetic, as well as the basic structures of governance to be able to vote and fully engage. But I know some communities won't care about those things either, and we accept them like the Amish. Your children, your choice has real meaning to us, and I have no doubt for those children who choose a different path upon their majority, there will be private assistance to help them find their own way.

The monopoly by the state on schooling has been the deep heart of cultural subversion, and while we envision the wholesale transformation of what exists to offer a better and more culturally affirming alternative, the reality is competition in ideas is healthy, and state mandated monopolies most certainly are not.

XI: No Wage Tax

With the eleventh right, we take a bold new step toward liberating our people toward greater social mobility by asserting you have the inviolable right to keep whatever salary you earn while working in the employ of someone else. Our desire is to see the advancement of our people and there is no surer way to promote success than to ensure you keep the fruits of your labor.

To be very clear, wage taxes mean those moneys earned in service to someone else. Income taxes, which is profit or loss from business enterprises, is a different category altogether, as the IRS has occasionally acknowledged, and these are not exempt but in the spirit of this amendment, an amount equal to double the median income will be automatically exempt for business owners so the same benefit is equally applied to both proprietors and employees.

We hope to encourage a society where saving is rewarded and where you can, if you so choose, largely exist outside the realm of the state so long as you adhere to the basic laws of the land and don't cause too much trouble. Compare this to the American or Canadian tax codes that basically reward the ultra-wealthy through loopholes and complexity, attack the poor with threats of punishment and retribution, and keep the middle class stuck.

New Albion doesn't believe you should work to pay for the state in debt bondage, and we put it here into law so that no tyrant in the future can force this of you as we labor under now.

XII: No Homestead Tax

The final right directly complements the removal of wage taxes and that is that we prohibit any land tax upon your primary residence where you live and potentially work. The days where property owners essentially are paying the state as landlord come to an end in New Albion. Your family home is yours without any presumption of a tax burden. So long as your homestead or farmstead is your actual primary residence, actively worked, and does not represent land speculation, you'll be free and clear.

When you read what the people who currently run our society have written for a hundred years now, they have consistently identified the desire to collectivize agriculture and remove people from the land as goals to decrease individual self-sufficiency, increase state dependency, and remove the ability to offer resistance to their social programming agenda. As New Albion has often noted, they see country folk as the primary threat, and we have seen ever rising efforts to compel people off the land through elevation of taxes, environmental burdens, and restrictions of property used to break the people's ability to choose.

In this one amendment, New Albion erases the suggestion of serfdom and makes you and your family freeholders of the land where you live. Obviously, this cannot be used to claim more than you use, and these protections do not apply inherently to business or corporate use, but what it does is ensure your family will always have your home so long as you choose.

Taken together, the eleventh and twelfth rights represent a sea change in the relationship between the state and the citizen where sovereignty is returned, wealth is preserved, and the balance of authority shifts back to the people. Chapter Eleven of this book and the planned fourth book will go much more deeply into the tax implications, but much like the original American model, we're going to be looking at sales taxes, excise taxes, user fees, tariffs, and foreign visitor duties upon services to cover the revenue gap. The math works, and the freedom works even better.

These twelve amendments reflect New Albion's Bill of Rights which has been designed to deliberately defend all that our ancestors preserved those two centuries before with valuable updates designed to anticipate new challenges to our sovereignty emerging in our technologically evolving world, to preserve the family and the right to choose dissenting paths, and to see the material backing ultimately necessary for these rights to have anything other nominal meaning actually protected.

The eventual adoption of these will be the first act of the New Albion government, but in all that we do, we already adhere to these principles as the basis upon which we challenge the legitimacy of the existing American and Canadian regimes. To the north, these rights are not even presumed to exist, which is a very sad situation we will work to rectify. For Americans, we have seen our First, Second, Fourth, Fifth, and Tenth Amendment rights violated repeatedly, and I would ask if a government actively ignores half its own laws, how can we still pretend that it is somehow legitimate?

I would argue in the strongest terms that it is not, and as what we do in New Albion is to essentially build a government for and by the people, the *Atlantic Charter* represents a faithful extension and superior development of the ideas that have served us so well and which our governments sadly look to undo as they seek to take control. They employ the tyranny of the majority to advocate their ability to harness numbers essentially in service of ignorance claiming this has a greater moral mandate than defending values whose obvious import will be self-evident and beneficial to all.

We live our values in New Albion. Our rights are simple; We expect our people to be held to account, the definitions are honest, and we are flexible to adapt for families and individuals, which is the greatest localization we can possibly manage. With a foundation such as this whereby the people are not just protected, but are required to protect themselves, we can realize our monarchy of excellence, take on greater responsibility, and advance once more our civilization.

Chapter Three: Bill of Responsibilities

Through no fault of their own, the Framers of the American Constitution have found so much of their work undone through the combined efforts of foreign spending, an activist judiciary, and a complacent legislature. Although we nominally have the Bill of Rights to protect us, the armies of lawyers which will never be permitted to exist in New Albion have altered, augmented, and amended the protections we had into mere shadows of their former weight and have literally worked through policy to restructure the very population, culture, and even history of our country to justify their usurpation of our liberties and sovereignty. This movement exists because of not just their malfeasance, but the learned ignorance which has been inculcated upon us to facilitate the deception about the intention for our rights.

There is no substitute for an active and engaged populace to defend its basic prerogatives and its future, and we have tried our very best to not just encourage, but almost require such for our society in how we balance individual rights with greater responsibility and less state intervention against self-destructive actions. We are well aware our biggest criticisms are going to come from those who come beating their sackcloths complaining of all those who will not be taken care of, and they will make the same appeal to feelings they always do to try to circumvent the requirements of reason. We have seen what happens when the state tries to be all things to all people; a tyranny of the mediocre conducted by the cynical. Our best effort to contest this trend inherently will require a renewed commitment to excellence, self-awareness, and accountability. In creating the *Atlantic Charter*, we made the decision to enhance our case by presenting those responsibilities we hoped to address with this work and to which we commend our descendants to continue if this society we imagine is to endure and prosper.

Speaking across the years of history into a world unknown is an impossible task, yet we must try so that our descendants have the benefit of understanding not just what are doing with New Albion, but the reasons why we have done so, trusting that well-educated people in the future may learn from the examples that we expect will prove analogous to their challenges should human society endure. As we believe reason remains constant and nature is predictable, such efforts are an act of immense loyalty to bind the generations that follow us as we try to save our civilization and we hope you have the grace to improve and amend our understanding which is coming out of a most challenging and compromised age.

As much as we think of posterity, we must make clear our responsibilities are specifically drawn up for the challenges of today. In accordance with our desire to be sincere about what must be done for this civilization to endure, the people to recover themselves, and sanity to resume, these objectives are ones we commend to our nation of New Albion to pursue always in service to our people.

I. Defend the traditional nuclear and extended family, honoring men and women as indispensable partners.

There are two models in existence for how society should function. The first is rooted in organic connections bound by blood and affection in equal measure, which unites men and women to create life and nurture that to prosperity and potential, and encourages this unity as the center of society and the means by which we invest our very nature, our genetic legacy, into a future we cherish.

By contrast, the model which we have been manipulated into adopting with greater speed and frequency sees men and women as competitors, disaffected individuals competing in the same race, and to be set against one another with the state inserted as an indispensable referee, most often working to subsidize women and degrade men as means to disrupt nature and alienate both genders.

New Albion recognizes the war between the sexes, a most unhealthy and unnatural creation, must end with a truce and a reconciliation that admits neither men nor women are better than one another, but instead explores the depth of our different natures, seeks to allow the fullest expression of these differences, and encourages an organic society to evolve which fulfills both.

It is no accident that even before we discuss the individual, we placed the family as our highest aspiration. The key to liberty has ever been defense of the sovereign household, and from the King of New Albion to the king of your own castle, we believe strongly that families reconnecting between sexes and generations will cause more good than a thousand laws and proclamations.

The family is the smallest social unit capable of self-replication, and as we face a challenging world, we remind ourselves that New Albion recognizes our people as our most precious asset, and we seek to create a culture and society that venerates life and celebrates the passage of our days and the introduction of new beings as the future of our people, not the replacement of new pieces in a system as we presently admit with our disloyal policies.

It will be for later volumes to flesh out the manifestation of these impulses, which should be considered more for guidance than as static rules, but we envision using the state to help strengthen the family as we have done with the preceding rights restricting the worst practices of the state. We will also look for opportunities in the future to encourage and promote family growth and parents being more involved with their children as well as older generations and extended family as socially desirable.

II: Preserve individual liberty as enumerated and beyond

As proud as we are of the Bill of Rights included in the *Atlantic Charter*, we recognize that other rights exist which should be defended even if we struggle to always clearly articulate how they are defined or how they can best be defended. A core practice we have adopted is trying to develop a culture that answers these questions rather than an interventionist state, so we include this provision here as a reminder that where possible, it is better to err in defense of liberty and to proceed cautiously.

Even a cursory study of history reveals that the biggest cause of death and deprivation has been the wholesale murder of people by their own governments, and we are not so vain as to assume any society is intrinsically exempt from these influences. As we watch parents lose their children because of a refusal to mutilate their sexual organs, how can we pretend America became any less insane, even if the path we took to get there was more twisted? We encourage our people to defend their rights vigorously, to defend them as required, and preserve older rights even as you add new ones. An inefficient society is superior to a meat grinder of human transformation, and this conservative outlook which does not so easily lend itself to the utopian excitement which might more readily inspire, has shown itself far more durable.

We have tried to help encourage this policy by ensuring rights cannot be removed under New Albion, but that new rights may be added by a 75% majority. That ability must be preserved to the people so that we may evolve our societies in peace, or at least try to restrain the need to go to the wars that have proven so destructive in our past. When we look at the West in 2020, we see a society whose worldwide population proportion has shrunk by two-thirds, and has become compressed and overrun by a world which expands into riches which we facilitated but knew not how to defend. Hopefully, the future chooses more wisely and carefully if we are to renew ourselves in New Albion and elsewhere.

III: Put people first above systems or ideology

The common denominator in all that has gotten America, Canada, and the entirety of Western Civilization in Europe and beyond is we have lived for too long in just our heads and not in the actual world where we reside. I say this because we have fought generations of wars over systems, over the superiority of ideas or our respective identities, and have tried to bring our systems to the world believing that we could create some perfect solution for us and everyone. The reality is we hurt a lot of people, especially ourselves, and for both the good and bad intentions of the process, the entire exercise has been profoundly unnatural and has risen to become an existential threat to our very being.

Whether capitalism versus communism, men versus women, different denominations, or whatever duality you so choose, we have fought and bled enough over these questions, and have allowed ourselves to be controlled as we keep dividing into tribes to resolve these conflicts. It may be we cannot ever fully escape this linguistic and mental limitation, but we implore you to try in

New Albion and escape this mental trap of positivism that has so enmeshed us in the West. My earlier works cover this in more detail, but positivism which postulates there is one final answer to be found in this world of man is a trap that has killed more people than any other single thought in human history.

Have grace instead to seek answers, but recognize that life like nature is cyclical, and that our people follow these cycles. Celebrate the young, respect the mature, venerate the elder, and instead of fitting people to some premade system, take the time to know our people and build structures that work for them. Use the state, use the market, make new solutions, and recognize that the right answer will often be messy and incomplete. Such is the joy of life, and if we could celebrate that instead of reducing ourselves to be just a fraction of ourselves so that we can fit some external designation, how much happier, safer, and more successful might we finally be?

We are proud nationalists, and we must always remember our people are our most precious asset. In whom we protect, whom we honor, and whom we choose to admit, never forget this. People are not just interchangeable parts to service our minds, but within each man or woman hides a universe of possibility, and help them to find that if we want to reach our highest potential.

IV: To honor our history, heritage, and homeland

Only from experience can we most fully understand who we are and what we achieve. Each of us stand on the shoulders of other giants, and we should never forget or overlook that responsibility. Even as we may be humbled in our own actions, let us use our faculties to build upon and glorify their achievements, trusting in the method of the West as articulated in New Albion of reason, nature, grace, and loyalty to be faithful servants to our past and through such, also our future.

As the third book will make clear, we look to our European ancestry heavily to guide this project. Everything New Albion does is informed by the best understanding we can gather of what actually happened in our past, a challenge to discern in any age, and what works best. We seek to understand who we are by the things we have done, and recognize that nature applies as much to humanity as any other species, seeing the uniqueness of different peoples as an organic process shaped by environment and developed through culture. Individuals will vary, but we want to find a self of ourselves that will always be part creation and partly intrinsic.

We honor tradition and hope to see it become a bigger part of our lives. People need to belong, and in an age where technology advances so quickly that it isolates, the challenge of connecting to one another and using our roots to find ways to be sure advances serve us rather than simply use to meet their requirements is not trivial. We want our people to be happy, which might sound silly, but is a vital consideration that only is possible if we know who we are and use all our talents to understand the world around us through connecting to one another today and from yesteryear.

V: To serve as refuge for Christians and Whites against persecution

Based upon the many conversations we had concerning the adoption of these responsibilities, this was, by far, the most controversial provision and yet, perhaps the most essential one for our time. We live in a world where people are actively being persecuted by the state for postulating any authority external to the government and those under its control has validity, and such, we see the persecution of those who speak for moral excellence, fidelity to their people, or honoring the old ways accelerate daily.

It is no accident the most potent voices in support of a better path and those people most inclined to speak to such values are now essentially defined as the enemies of the culture. Here in North America, to be very specific, that means that we have seen the targeting of Whites, Christians, heterosexuals, and rural folk for scorn, derision, replacement, and economic boycott. As many key thinkers of New Albion embrace these values, we ask the future to be mindful of their plight and seek to help as they best see fit.

For as much as we recognize freedom of belief, and for as willing as we have been to integrate those who are not of European origin who want to share our values and be a party to our culture, we learned the hard lesson which you must remember that our ways will not work for all people and should we lose our majority, we will be persecuted and erased regardless of how kindly we choose to act toward others. Such is an axiom of history that people protect their own, and as such, New Albion should be mindful that as nationalists charged with preserving the seed of the West, you may be called upon for extraordinary measures to preserve those with whom you share meaningful bonds.

As we conceive this project, we built our borders and our accession process to protect people who fit these definitions along with allies and to the mutual benefit of all included. What this means in other times is something to be determined because we do not intend to mean the unsustainable altruism of bringing people ill-suited to our society into our midst, but it does mean having considered openness based upon self-awareness and an honest appraisal of the world of the present and with whom we can mutually benefit.

We should also make clear that as this is being adopted, we envision our founding to be an attractant for people of European origin and Christian background to be the founding stock of our country, and to those especially who come from American or Canadian areas outside our borders, we plan on an initial right of return which we think will prove wise for the long term as well, and potentially should be extended to Europe and similarly settled places and populations as a means to show our moral leadership for the civilization we hope to resurrect.

VI: To ensure our children have a better future, and that our future is for them.

This sixth responsibility represents our inherent obligation to the future generations to follow by which we must measure all our actions of the day. Returning to the importance of the family, one of the most damaging developments of a state-sovereign rather than family led model has been that as disconnected individuals, we have so often developed policy that thinks only of immediate benefit or short-term gains and ignored the world we are leaving for our children.

The generation that exists at the time of this writing is the first in human history in many centuries to enjoy a less prosperous standard of living than the one which preceded us, a sad commentary on the moral decay that is rife in America and Canada. We want to make sure this never happens again, and so we instruct our society to make legislation that doesn't just preserve the past, and protect the future, but considers the implications for the future and for those who cannot yet speak for their world.

As skeptical as some of us are, for many reasons, about concerns expressed about the environment and larger questions that impact all humanity, we must apply our own honest logic to making independent appraisals of the future based on truth and nature instead of ideology and patronage, and be unafraid to show leadership based upon an independent path that speaks to the world and honors our people.

We want to make policies that invest heavily in our children, in the families that birth and sustain them, and in being examples for which they can be proud. Many of us now feel like we live in a lost generation, having made unhappy compromises to survive a troubling world, and our hope at many times is they will live in such a healthier place they will not have to understand all we had to overcome as we will have acted better as their stewards in handing them a far better future than the one we've now inherited.

VII: Seek public consensus to forge a common culture.

One of the largest struggles which we have dealt with in society is that we who believe in virtue have understood the very imposition of such values, even with the best of intentions, often undoes the intended impact. As such, we have worked very hard to try to find a persuasive and voluntary way toward the future, and regardless of whether or not we are brought to conflict by those who oppose us, it was vital to us to offer a solution that allowed for an amicable separation.

Fundamentally, we believe in using reason rather than violence to advance human civilization. While we are not pacifists, we know that the way forward should most often not be to force compliance, but instead to develop consensus on issues and allow great latitude to encourage exploration and development. We tried very hard in these laws to identify those areas where the state had to engage for this effort to succeed, and equally vigorously to remove the state or decentralize efforts in those places where we hope to reinvigorate the freedom and potential of the people.

The third book is devoted in much greater depth toward how we accomplish this, and we want to encourage people to understand themselves, and exert independence and interdependence in a way that fulfills the vision and imperative gifted to us by those who settled North America as the vision of what a pan-European civilization in service to the good might accomplish. We will ask more questions than we offer answers, but we recognize the best trait of New Albion is a willingness to reopen critical inquiry and to apply what we learn about the world to ourselves as well.

You will also note that in how we have structured the government, we have made it so different levels have to work together, certain authorities are deliberately blended, and the finances are divided to encourage greater cooperation but less partisanship. A ship cannot ever reach the shore if it is does not move in one direction.

VIII: Discover truth through the use of reason

Twenty years ago, it would have been absurd to include this provision as a foundational imperative, but the eighth responsibility reminds us we can only serve our people and sustain our state if we build our foundations in truth.

There is a long and somewhat sordid history of how those who have visions of the future where they want to assume control have learned to engineer language, culture, and media to promote falsehood and relativity in a way to degrade reason. If the topic interests you, learn about the pernicious influence of the Frankfurt School and be vigilant against such perfidy, but the core of their argument can be reduced to they never allow you to assert A is unequal to B. Through many different tricks, some of which are surprisingly compelling by reframing arguments, they constantly push people to surrender their reason and their ability to make judgments and arguments. Once they win those victories, then they use force in many guises to bully their opponents into voluntary or involuntary submission. These deceivers are evil.

The way to beat them, as they will recur, and to ensure a healthy civilization is to never retreat from using reason to assert when A is unequal to B, and build this nation upon the basis of such truth as you can defend, not those feelings which are inherently subjective. Explore them all you like, as an essential part of the human experience, but recognize that empathy alone is no basis upon which to build the foundation of any social effort, and require the sensitivity of concern to be matched with sensibility in equal or greater measure.

All of our achievements come from our willingness to build upon what we can identify as true, and be unafraid to examine nature, of man himself and the world at large, with the same critical nature. Only then can we enjoy a better reality through self-knowledge.

IX: Exercise responsible stewardship over nature

Some things are irreplaceable. We live in an age where many men use numbers in such a way to suggest one resource may be used as substitute for another unto infinity. These economists only see the utility of a substance, one function of what it accomplishes, and overlook that it may serve many purposes that are interconnected in ways we do not fully apprehend.

As such, we want to look at our environment at several levels, and this is as true of our society of men as it is the wilderness with which we are blessed to coincide. We need to consider the macro as carefully as the micro, and in all of our planning, try to assess the long-term impact as deeply as the short-term. By no means do we advocate idleness, but instead we tend to think about integration into our nature as a part of who we are in mutual sustenance.

Nature is neither a resource to be exploited or a preserve to be set aside, but an active part of who we are and with which we should engage so our understanding is as much visceral and experiential and intellectual, trusting that we will live in these lands which will sustain us and with whom we will grow together.

Unique amongst nations, we embrace a belief that we do not just preserve nature, but that nature shapes us. As New Albion develops just as we understand we are a people apart, we must also always remember that unique peoples require unique lands and we must be very honest with ourselves about what places are and are not best suited for us to discover our fullest potential.

X: Provide for the public health, safety, and well-being

These final three responsibilities include basic instruction for good governance which seem self-evident, but which are included anyway as no less important. If we have learned nothing else from these challenging times, it is to assume nothing about how others will interpret why certain provisions are included.

The job of the state properly identified is to work for the benefit of its people. There is inherently a feedback relationship between the two that will always have some tension, but in a healthy construct, the state makes better people who are happier and more fulfilled, who in turn provide for the safety and security of this mutually beneficial project.

Essential to this outcome is working to ensure the public remains healthy, which means that harmful ideas should be contested, nutrition and sound development encouraged, and criminality actively confronted. In difficult times such as the onset of New Albion, I expect justice to be swifter, involvement to be greater, and conflicts to be more numerous. But as we find better pathways and adopt them for our mutual benefit, we aim for domestic tranquility and the opportunity for a simpler and more honest way of being.

XI: Avoid entanglements, needless conflict, and debt usury

George Washington gave America most excellent advice which it proceeded abruptly to ignore leading to the sorry situation we face today. New Albion is a nation apart, and we should avoid entangling ourselves in any permanent relationship with foreign powers save as absolutely necessary to forestall the imposition of more permanent threats to our homeland.

North America is blessed to be segregated from the dangers of the Old World through two oceans providing material separation which allows our moral exploration. We do not want to see the rise of a power that threatens this cause, and so we should work to support national determination as the Monroe Doctrine suggested to ensure our continent remains a land apart, sustain a navy capable of enforcing this goal, but otherwise eschew any presumed responsibility elsewhere.

We can be a home to Europeans, but we are not Europe and they are not us. They are proud to be their distinctive identities, where we are a combination of their bravest children which makes us something new and unique. We are greater than the sum of our parts and must transcend the conflicts they once fought. No more brothers' wars, as it is sometimes said, and we hope to achieve that with our nonviolent model in North America.

Central to that is eliminating the role of usury and debt lending. Banking has been the means by which so many societies have been undone, the hidden hand manipulating countries against one another, and we would better to live in honest poverty sustaining ourselves and protecting ourselves through mutual assured destruction than to allow the bankers to determine the future of New Albion. They are the dark heart of possession that destroys all value, that uses our children as their victims, and we must rebuke them and see they never gain control over our destiny.

XII: Keep secure the nation in faith and fidelity.

New Albion is a gift which we will have to pay dearly to create, and as such, our fatherland deserves your loyalty. In return, like any proper liege, hold it to account to serve your interest and this honest and righteous exchange may very well last happily for many centuries. We have the right people and the right land for something truly remarkable.

It is an odd admonition to offer as a radical literally advocating for revolutionary thought in a trying time, but please consider most thoughtfully if you should live in a more tranquil time how many ways in which things can go wrong. Peace is never exciting, but war is a hell which destroys so much with the likelihood of no benefit but those external to the entire conflict. We face those uncertainties here at the origin, but should you enjoy the blessings of peace and liberty, fight to preserve them and go see the world, in your mind's eye or in real experience if you imagine any better.

Western Civilization is a gift which may yet exit this world. New Albion exists to ensure it does not, and our patriots who act bravely to remember this will be heroes in any time, whether we succeed or not. We honored our legacy, which we all do by honoring our sacred responsibilities across these generations.

Chapter Four: Criminal Law

The basic orientation of criminal law in New Albion is to improve upon the existing foundation of Common Law by expediting justice, simplifying the legal code, providing for both flexibility and severity in sentencing as determined most appropriate by the people themselves, and making what has often been a field riddled by technicalities into something swifter and clearer.

Our presumption remains that individuals must be presumed innocent absent evidence to the contrary and that the burden of proof rests with the prosecution in any trial. Evidence must be legally obtained in accordance with best legal practices, and in full accord with the various privacy provisions enumerated within the *Atlantic Charter*. Such protections already nominally exist within existing American legal practice, but they are strengthened and more clearly codified herein.

Where the New Albioner system diverges from the American equivalent is in how professionalized the system will be. We do not presume the need for an attorney because we have sufficiently simplified the system where we do not believe one is necessary. In both our criminal and civil code, the assumption is made that a person of sound mind and body can represent themselves. We want the accused individuals to offer their own defense based upon their testimony, to accelerate the flow of legal traffic in most cases.

However, to ensure effective representation where desired, there will be access to attorneys available for those accused of crimes whose verdicts could potentially include incarceration or other penalties. The complex nature of certain cases requires this capacity as a means to ensure a fair trial.

How this manifests in our direct form of justice is simpler. Essentially, we are going to disband the bar association as anything other than an informal credential by allowing anyone who so chooses to practice law. People may represent themselves or bring whomever they so choose to serve as their advocate, keeping in mind they bear full responsibility for the choice.

A digression as to why this is being done might be helpful. As we observe in most Western legal systems, the progressive bureaucratization of law has essentially served as a barrier to entry for people seeking to enter this field, to artificially inflate cost and time involved, and has been directly responsible for the voluminous amount of laws considered as precedent and procedure. In accordance with our desire for simplicity and honesty, New Albion has a far simpler code and conduct, and best practices will be far less formalized to open up the Court.

Such action is not without precedent. As late as fifty years ago, one did not require a Juris Doctorate to practice law. The Bar did not always have such power as it now wields. Intelligent lay people could and did win cases, a practice which still continues today in New Hampshire and a few other random locations, but which we have seen lawyers themselves seek to undo at every opportunity.

It is no secret that lawyers have been at the heart of the rise of the massive bureaucracy that so cripples America from moving forward, so it will probably be no surprise that in both criminal and civil law, New Albion does much to restrain this influence. We do not want law to be difficult and complex so people live off it, we want it to be clear and simple so our people do not run afoul of it which is our goal in the high trust society we hope to create.

For that same reason, New Albion takes an entirely novel approach to sentencing. We have no guidelines to constrain or commend certain penalties for specific crimes. The decision for sentencing shall be made by the Count, who being ultimately accountable to the mayors selecting him, is indirectly linked to public opinion as to what constitutes fair judgment. We have seen so often that people committing truly heinous acts get treated lightly due to overly precise laws, and we have also frequently seen the opposite where onerous sentences are imposed for minor infractions. A more flexible approach is needed where we grant leeway to the court to make better decisions.

A concern which one could reasonably express in this system is that as the Count holds the office of Sheriff essentially as well as Judge that the state will represent both the prosecution and the arbiter. However, we envision this will be mitigated as we assume law enforcement professionals will exist from a chief deputy downward who will functionally enact the day to day action of investigating crime, and through the effort of the district attorney which will be a professional office that operates autonomously from the Count's office in accordance with law. In reality, neither the Court nor the district attorney has never been as separated from politics as people would imagine, and this system increases efficiency while recognizing the need for some walls of separation to exist at the county level to ensure a fair trial.

Furthermore, as guaranteed by the seventh right, each person is always ensured access to a trial by jury for any infraction where possible incarceration may result. The specific exemption imagined here is for minor offenses of a trivial nature that come before the court for essentially arbitration purposes as there are a number of disputes which exist in a grey area between civil and criminal law that may arise, and we do not presume these cases require the burden of a jury trial. Twelve people selected at random from amongst the citizenry of that county shall be selected, and individuals shall be presumed to make themselves ready to serve as a civic duty in this capacity. We are not going to have jury selection drama to cherry pick individuals who judge trials, which is another excess of this system, as we assume as a matter of principle all our citizens are capable of exercising sound judgment so long as they are recognized to be of clear mind.

Subpoenas, warrants to appear, will continue and be used to ensure that accurate accounting of justice continues, and are compelled as a civic duty in service to both the accused and the state.

The Accounting may choose to adopt a legal code of best practices that it finds most useful for the conduct of these operations and as guidelines for how to operate a trial as a matter of common procedure. Such protocol must be in accordance with all protected rights of the citizenry, satisfy the requirements for a speedy trial, and also ensure the right of appeal.

For those convicted of an offense, they shall have the right of appeal for either the sentencing or upon the judgment rendered. Appellees should be aware that the Appeals Court, consisting of three mayors randomly chosen from within the county jurisdiction will have the power to enhance as well as restrain sentencing. They may also, if requested to review the judgment, increase the severity of the crime or decrease such as evidence warrants.

Our criminal legal system will maintain the practice of not permitting double jeopardy, which is to say being tried twice for the same offense. We will also end the practice that currently exists in the United States where a person has someone been charged with two different crimes at two different levels for the same basic offense. As example of the principle, we have sometimes seen how a defendant will be charged with a violent act as a state crime and perhaps a weapons violation as a federal crime and tried separately. This power grab, usually conducted by the higher agency as a means of coercion and overreach will not exist in New Albion both because all offenses except high crimes against the state are tried at the county level, and because we are explicitly forbidding that practice. All crimes resulting from a single incident shall be tried together and adjudicated in concert.

We also will continue the practice whereby one cannot be arrested without cause, cannot be held indefinitely without being charged, and has the right to face one's accusers. These actions are described in plain language from the desire to de-mystify the legal terms such as habeus corpus being described to a basic expectation the people can rely upon to ensure honest application of justice.

In short, the legal system will operate much like what you know except it will be faster, more direct, devoid of the technicality driven bombast, and will have a few more protections for the defendant while allowing for more flexibility in sentencing. We fully expect there will be some time needed to develop a streamlined process in full, but taking lawyers out of the equation as the masters of the system and returning justice to the people is a major step in the right direction.

Since we have described in some detail how the legal system will work, the second half of this chapter is devoted to identifying the basic categories of criminal offense. Unless charged with one of these specific crimes, no citizen of New Albion may be incarcerated. Such prohibition does not extend to military crimes which may be conducted by separate tribunal in accordance with their own code.

The recognized criminal acts of New Albion are:

Abduction – This category includes the kidnapping of an individual against their will, forcible restraint or imprisonment, or all cases where a person is held hostage against their will.

Arson – Using fire or any other deliberate substance to destroy public or private property falls under this heading as would most acts of deliberate destruction with a special emphasis on the larger threat of contagion endangering the public safety.

Assault – When a physical attack is committed against one person by another, this constitutes assault, and should a weapon be used, this will be deemed aggravated assault.

Burglary – Theft of public or private property accomplished by use of a weapon as the most dangerous form of theft because of the elevated risk of violence including usage of such falls here.

Larceny – Larceny represents the theft of personal or private property, sometimes called robbery, without the use of a weapon that would include categories like breaking and entering.

Manslaughter – Manslaughter represents those cases where death or serious harm is inflicted due to acts that represent criminal negligence leading to such injury.

Murder – Any action which results in the willful, intentional, and deliberate death of another person constitutes murder.

Perjury – The swearing of a false oath before the Court constitutes perjury and is subject to severe penalty.

Rape – An act of sexual violence whereby a person is forced to perform sexual acts without their consent, including all acts with persons under the proscribed age of consent, constitutes rape.

Theft – A broader category of theft exists for all crimes which involve other means of obtaining property beyond direct stealing, but which clearly are in violation of property rights.

Trafficking – The crime of illegally moving people or illicit goods within and without of the country which also includes human elements such as illegal migration and sex rings, but also the importation of illegal drugs.

Trespass – The unlawful violation of property rights of an individual who has so informed the offender to remain away is a trespass violation which may be charged.

Lastly, as an independent issue for the Crown, there exists a charge of *High Treason* to be tried by the King for kingdom offenses and by the Prince for principal offenses against any official of the government found guilty of bribery, embezzlement, espionage, sedition or related crimes against the state and people. In extreme cases where violent terrorism is conducted resulting in mass death, these charges may also be extended to guilty public parties as a Crown prerogative for national security to be used sparingly.

Having laid out the basic tenets of the prosecutable offenses, we recognize that other crimes will fit under these headings, and want to talk just a little about how we envision the weight of charges. Our society relies upon people to resolve their own issues where possible, and we do not want the Court overly burdened. We also, in accordance with our publicly stated responsibilities, do not want the public's health, safety, or confidence damaged, so for crimes committed against society, expect harsh sentencing.

It is also worth noting we deliberately have not restricted sentencing to incarceration as we believe it is reasonable to have more expansive punishment considered in cases. For a serial rapist, as one example, castration would be permissible under our system. It is for the people themselves through their elected representatives to determine the severity of judgment they think appropriate, but we do not restrain ourselves because our highest job is to protect our people from predation, and instead of burdening our citizens with the cost of incarceration, we will consider alternative options to both permanently eliminate recidivism possibilities, and discourage criminal behavior.

While New Albion agrees with protection for the individual and giving every reasonable opportunity for the innocence of the accused to be revealed, we also recognize our duty as a state is to ensure that we develop a society where crime is low, trust is high, and justice is fair. If we seem harsher in our execution, it because we have learned through sorry demonstration that when injustice is encouraged to proliferate and the very system of legality itself becomes a trading house, then the people become hurt, indifferent, and society retreats into itself.

Having worked for some years as a legal clerk, I would add as personal observation that there is no reason we cannot speed up this process, reduce the paperwork, render fair sentences far more efficiently, and for complex cases, allow bail to see prosecution only happens when the state is ready to make their argument. But for those who we find guilty, we do not want to have our jails be revolving doors – we want people to learn the lesson and to never come back. If that requires severity, it is a lesser and fairer price to pay than to force the public to tolerate lawlessness and disorder.

Those twelve laws above and the thirteenth royal check to protect the nation and people are our legal code, reflect our values of honesty and simplicity, and are the heart of justice in New Albion.

Chapter Five: Civil and Family Law

Let's begin this chapter by acknowledging that there are many issues involved with civil law, that trying to cover all these is beyond the scope and purpose of this document, and that such discussion being particular to the question of what is being settled falls under the broad concern of judicial function which New Albion acknowledges as right and proper, but for which future practice will evolve to accomplish these ends. Having begun with that necessary caveat, we have some thoughts on how we want the civil and family law practices to evolve differently than the current American system.

While Americans have historically enjoyed excellent protections in criminal court, thanks to the Bill of Rights, those closest to the legal profession have often come to see civil courts as a place where people who have money basically beat one another up until one pushes the other into submission. Although this observation might be highly cynical, anyone who has ever been party to a lawsuit may recognize the essential truth that our current system has this distasteful trait. We want to try to change this, and so we're going to simplify the legal procedures.

As with criminal law, we have removed the requirement for having a formal legal background to be involved. This is not an invitation to frivolity in terms of the legal process as we do not envision nearly as expansive a view of liability because we want to actively discourage a litigious culture which we see as not commensurate with a responsible or highly productive and trusting society. We want to restrain ourselves to those claims which are most salient.

Formally, we have removed the right of jury trials for civil procedure in the interests of removing a public inconvenience, and to accelerate the case load placed upon the Count in his capacity as Judge. A basic tenet of our legal code is any affairs related to civil trials shall be tried only in the place where an action happened, or for institutions interacting between one another, where the complainant has official residence.

As the nature of these disputes are often complex, the way our system will deal with these issues without becoming overly burdensome is to assign an arbiter to each case to attempt to resolve the issues at question between both parties through mediation. It is hoped these issues can frequently be resolved to mutual accord by this official of the Count, but if mediation proves inadequate, the parties can request a determination by the arbiter. Such decision as made by the arbiter will be legally binding, but may be appealed by either party to the Count.

If such an appeal is made for reconsideration, the Count will consider the case on the merits receiving the case of the plaintiff, complainant, and the summary and findings of the arbiter. Whatever final determination is made by the Count shall be binding, and at any point, a dispute between two parties may be resolved through mutually acceptable terms to conclude the case prior to resolution by the Count.

The goal of this system is to seek consensual solutions that do not tie up the government in negotiations between private actors. However, in cases which arise as in liability claims such as we see from time to time in malpractice where the parties are adversarial, we fully anticipate a sizable number of claims, especially in areas where there is a larger number of people to be considered. The arbiter represents the effort to stem the number of cases to a manageable amount, and should in most cases be presumed to be acting as the voice of the Count.

To restrain the unhelpful tendency for people to appeal until their terms improve, it is worth noting that should one party appeal to the Count a decision rendered by the arbiter, that party will bear responsibility for any additional court costs for the administration of questions, and should the Count affirm the decision of the arbiter, then a reduction in the settlement or increase in award may be considered specifically as warning for wasting the time of the court. Upon entering the Court, it is most important to recognize equity consists of three parties, the complainant, the plaintiff, and the public who is represented also by the Court, so if adjustments are made beyond the figures of the specific question, the Count is granted latitude to factor these decisions in a way the arbiter is not.

What we hope to accomplish is to have contractual disputes settled amicably through arbitration, discourage frivolous lawsuits, and see only those cases with the most merit occupy the time of the Count. To wit, the arbiter will also have the right to unilaterally dismiss specious claims, which may be appealed to the Count, but who will conduct a visual review rather than hearing, and decide whether or not to open the case at the cost to the claimant.

New Albion is not the United States or Canada. We genuinely do not envision a society as we have today where everyone is trying to sue everyone. Instead, we want to work things out through consensus, and when issues arise, instead of having volumes of case law and complex formulae, our arbiters and our Counts are empowered to act commonsensically to settle disputes.

This is an intentional and deliberate act to discourage the usage of the courts for all but the most challenging claims. The reality is when you give the state power to make decisions in every area, law grows in equal concert, and the people find themselves living as they do today under a series of decisions that make no sense in so many cases but build upon precedent after precedent. Stare decesis, or that which came before, is out the window as law will be localized, flexible to the situation, and will be rooted in the particulars of the case rather than strictly the previous judgments.

We've focused heavily on contracts and torts in the beginning, so we should now talk about issues related to civil rights. The same system applies for alleged violations of the *Atlantic Charter* where the arbiter will opine if any person was wronged and suggest first corrective measures, and then escalating punitive damages. The same appeals process applies.

The nature of legal questions is such that a degree of professionalization, given our advanced society, is inescapable, but as we consider the arbiter and its unique powers, we balance that by having this be an at-will position at all times whereby any County may fire or hire an arbiter for any reason. This is especially important because if we have a series of poor decisions being made, and the public outcry demands change, the elected mayors may well replace the Count who will have to be able to replace their civil servants in the court to be able to adjust operations.

Another concern that we are considering with this system is case load. It is not possible for the Count to complete all their mandated duties, especially in higher density areas, absent some assistance. One could make the valid criticism that the Count will, in most cases, end up being a rubber stamp for arbiters who take on the role judges play today. The best we can do to mitigate this is adopt civil legal practices that discourage use of the system and encourage sound contractual practices and shirk a litigious culture.

We want our system to be honest, to be tough but fair, to work to remedy genuine inequities, but to be austere in pushing aside those who waste the time of the state. The reality is many cases happen because there are lawyers looking to make a buck who persuade clients to file flimsy claims. We hope this system mitigates that risk by removing the attorneys from serving who are so inclined, and would even consider a system for rating professionals who could find access prohibited in a professional, although never a personal self-representation, capacity from civil court.

An important difference in New Albion is there is no right of appeal to a higher court than the Count for civil or family law. This would seem like an oversight in the American construct of law where issues about application of the rules arise through the various appellate courts to the Supreme Court. There are two big reasons we do not see that as necessary. The first is that as our judicial and legislative functions are combined in the office of the Count, we believe that the issues that arise will organically find resolution in the Accounting and any modification to either law or practice will be collaborative. The second reason is beyond the clearly stated criminal code of illicit offenses that applies everywhere in the land, we are deliberately encouraging areas to develop autonomous legal practices best in concert with the expectations of the citizenry.

Consider the problems of the American system or the Canadian as an alternative, where regulatory agencies are made again and again and assume centralized authority as a demand to harmonize the legal code across jurisdictions. While the benefit, in theory, is having universal rules and regulations, the tradeoff has been making it so the national government makes restrictions on every issue, and has devoted billions of dollars to multiple agencies telling you what you cannot do with what you own or with your entities to resolve disputes where the presumption that government knows best and the people have to listen.

Our view is the precise inverse. We accept different counties will adopt different laws which make sense because our people, economies, and environments are different. Much we will agree upon and voluntarily coordinate. Some things we can develop a common practice through legal decisions to do differently in certain areas. Only rarely do we want the government stepping in and trying to tell you how to live, and our system is structured that way which appears inefficient from the perspective of homogenizing the legal code, but is actually quite flexible in allowing the people of an area to determine what they want where they live.

Let's use the area of the environment to demonstrate the principle. The current approach is to use regulatory agencies to compel certain actions which themselves are subject to high level political considerations, highly susceptible to fraud and trading, and which even at best create blanket actions which cause division and contention. In New Albion, you're going to see regions adopt different ways of handling environmental questions, but the means of compliance will be not external agencies, but citizens suing for damage to their private property by environmental malfeasance, which is a legitimate claim, and where the settlement goes to those harmed and the court works to help the state encourage better action with a popular mandate. Let's pretend the court ignores people being harmed – it won't be very long until that person is replaced, and this process of placing judges within the process instead of beyond such is a highlight of why our system should create much greater accountability and flexibility.

No system is perfect, and there will be times where we want to agree on common standards which can be adopted by the Accounting, our parliament. Conversely, there will be things upon which we will have to agree to disagree, as this form of judicial federalism will irritate some who want a singular solution, but we submit that having latitude is necessary not just to bring us together, but to reflect the sovereign will of the people. It also worked much better for Canada and America than trying to force one party to take control with one vision over all else, and we fight that mindset not with the sterile promise of a better party, but structural reforms that ensure local control over key powers.

A final point on civil law concerns corporations. This will feature in the fourth book, but we are moving strongly toward denying corporate personhood because we believe that as a corporate structure is not subject to the same pressures and constraints as a human being, this vehicle has proven capable of destructive and harmful public acts undertaken precisely because the lack of culpability assumed to the operating board has rendered the decision making process flawed. We understand the value of protecting investment and investors as well as the need for some limitations on what cannot be reasonably anticipated, however, look for our legal process to evolve liability limitation for investors more toward specifically delineated actions rather than in sustenance of larger entities like the current corporate structure.

Such reform is part of a much larger rethink of business that will certainly not be ready on day one, but reflects a priority that our entrepreneurial system reflects our values and defend our people.

Having covered several key areas of civil law, let us consider now family law. Informed by the eighth right of parental sovereignty and family integrity, New Albion desires to have a far smaller legal presence in this area than the American system currently adopts.

Let us begin with the process of marriage and divorce. Marriage in our nation is specifically defined as a monogamous relationship between one man and one woman only for the purposes of sustaining a family. Only this relationship will be granted status as marriage with any social benefits that accrue, although any two or more people can form whatever corporate structures they like for the protection of joint assets. Divorce happens when either of the two parties files a request the marriage be resolved, requires no finding of fault, and allows no alimony to or from either party.

For too many years, we have allowed our courts to be caught up in this mess where complaints about feelings are used to justify moving money between partners and where judges who wear their emotions on their sleeves make decisions for families for which they should have no sanction. New Albion removes these questions entirely from our jurisdiction.

With regard to children and custody cases, it is assumed each parent has equal custodial rights and equal financial obligations. These rights are retained by both parents unless one parent is found guilty of a violent criminal act directly against the child or children in question, in which case they will lose custodial rights. In the event both parents are found so guilty, the custody shall pass to the nearest family member available, best possible volunteer, or a state designee if no other option is available. With the consent of both parents, one parent may be removed from custodial duties if so requested before the Court.

One important consideration is even in cases of criminal removal of rights, there remains no financial obligation assumed to the other parent, specifically because if we do not do this, long years of exploitation of the courts have revealed the frequency with which parents lie about their partner to achieve certain outcomes. There is no benefit to lying here or breaking apart a marriage, and we think these things will only strengthen that institution.

The state will not be involved with adoption other than to ensure those adopting children are married couples in good standing who are the only people who can legally adopt in New Albion. We want to strengthen the family as the strongest possible institution, and we are going to make sure our kids get the benefit of both a mother and a father in their lives.

Our nation makes no presumption on those who choose alternate lifestyle arrangements as the free exercise of association, but we do not offer any sanction to these actions between consenting adults either than to recognize such basic protection.

To those raised in a progressive environment believing that love and feelings are the purpose of marriage and relationships, these measures may seem heartless. But to the more mature mind who understands family must be protected from intrusion by the state, seek to protect children, and to encourage men and women to act intelligently about their reproductive and bonding behaviors, these values represent mainstream thinking that has worked for thousands of years and is a much needed return to sanity.

This system will be far smaller, far quicker, much less expensive to administer, and remove several layers of costly and invasive bureaucracy at multiple levels which has shown itself rife for misuse.

In both family and civil law, what we are attempting is to return power to the people, end control by lawyers and bureaucrats, and revitalize a culture of trust, integrity, and accountability.

Chapter Six: Structure and Accession

Having addressed the rights, responsibilities, and legal obligations of the citizenry, this bridge chapter lays out who makes up New Albion in terms of territory and people before offering a wider view of the governance plan as a whole.

The technical way that we describe what we are doing is to create a vertical separation of powers with more democratic and consensual based deliberation at the local levels and monarchic unifying efforts at the higher echelons. We want the benefit of strong leadership to bring our people together under one vision, but to allow many paths that fit the specific needs and desires of all those who reside here to find fulfillment as they choose in their locality.

Let us make abundantly clear we believe New Albion is the homeland for all citizens who currently reside in America or Canada and who reside in the Northeast. While we are building our foundations upon European culture and European peoples, this project we renew has always had other partners representing a valued minority, and we recognize their contribution. We believe in returning to the historic model of an 85/15 solution or better because we want to end this war over identity and that only becomes possible when one group's vision is adopted by all. Once this happens, while we will certainly exercise a much more rational immigration policy that focus on cultural homogeneity as the key factor, we will integrate all who stay and help resettle all those who find they better belong elsewhere.

A number of times, we have been asked to offer a specific geographic designation for where New Albion resides, and the short answer is that our model works much like the Electoral College does between the Federal and State governments, but we replicate a similar concept between the Counties and their respective States. Any state or province, called principalities by our system, wherein a majority of the counties request to be admitted into New Albion will be considered, and in those places where a single county or city so dominates the politics, we will work to effectuate peaceful and mutually agreeable separation.

Any principality whose primary area resides north of the 36th parallel on the continent of North America is welcome to join New Albion as a full and equal partner. If you draw a line from the southern border of Virginia west, that's pretty accurate for who we seek to include automatically. Our heartland is in the Atlantic Northeast, so we build outward from our developing group in Maine and New Hampshire to outreach our neighbors with this opportunity for a new beginning, and we will see where it takes.

The original vision planned to incorporate Maine, New Hampshire and Vermont from the United States with New Brunswick, Nova Scotia and, Prince Edward Island from Canada. As the idea was introduced in various places, we found support as well from Newfoundland, Quebec, and upstate New York, which we call Niagara who are trapped under democratic suppression by the city. For the moment, this is our core area, and for those looking for the most action, we work in these areas.

But in seeing the long-term potential for this project, there has been support throughout the Great Lakes and into the Great Plains for what we are trying, and as we want to preserve as much territory as we logically can and as many people who understand the challenges ahead, so the vision has deliberately developed in a more expansive manner. We know we are the first to seriously offer an alternative, and we want to unite whoever fits with us.

Most importantly, as we watch the political breakdown happening in America today, and to a lesser extent seeing the push for autonomy in Canada as is now not just present in Quebec, but Alberta as well, we see how county governments as is happening in Virginia and other places are literally preparing to have potential conflict with their state capitals, and this trend can only accelerate given the polarization, identity politics, and the compulsion being forced on the people.

New Albion proposes a radically different approach for organization, and that's how we ask people to join with us. We don't fight over DC, but work county by county to encourage people to walk away. If we seek office, it is in our towns, counties, and from our sheriffs, because we want a world where sovereignty is mostly present in the community, the complete opposite of what everyone else has offered for the last two hundred years. This is the path to peace, and we pursue it vigorously.

It is not lost on anyone who makes these suggestions the improbability that simply walking away will be permitted. Although, the more of us who decide we are out, the more difficult it will be to stop this effort, and that's why we support other movements evolving by people who have different identity, or who have different motivating ideas, to find the fulfillment of their own vision in an American Divorce where we recognize despite our many and irreconcilable differences, we also gain nothing from trying to all control the corruption at the center. Speaking to that, if we do effectuate separation and are attacked, we always retain as an inherent right the choice of sovereignty and self-defense.

Time will reveal our map to us. We may end up a sliver on the Atlantic Coast. We may end up the upper Northeast. We may include the Great Lakes. We may get to the Pacific. Those choices are for the people to make. A final comment before we talk about the sovereign units of New Albion is for those who live below the boundary. Should a political entity so residing, which is geographically contiguous to our land, seek accession with the clearly expressed will of a majority of the counties, we may consider such action. In saying this, I can imagine states like Tennessee, North Carolina, and South Carolina potentially wanting to be included, or I can equally imagine them as the foundation of something novel in Dixie. That choice, as everywhere, is for locals to make, but we are always willing to listen to our neighbors.

New Albion has four basic units of government which are the town, the county, the principality (state/province), and the kingdom (national). While this system is arranged deliberately to convert the existing political subdivisions and assets in the least disruptive manner possible, we have a few provisions about what constitutes the three smaller subdivisions which must be discussed.

Our political orientation is toward the strong decentralization of power and having governing bodies which are held to account by the citizens. As part of this, and as a movement inspired by putting just as much emphasis on our lands as our people, we deliberately want to prevent the drift toward democratic despotism which happened by having too many people in too few places. It is accurate to say we actively push for smaller rather than bigger because we believe people exercise their better nature when they reside in places where they know more people, can exert greater trust, and can wield influence in their towns.

Applying that logic to the town, which is the smallest legal jurisdiction in New Albion, we had a number of conversations about how large a settlement could become before it was beyond accountability. No serious person who lives in a city of a million plus people thinks their government answers to individuals, but we think they should. As such, one of the first changes New Albion will require is we will not permit any cities to have a greater population than 100,000 people. For those places impacted, we will divide the existent cities by neighborhoods, which could be as small as 500 citizens if so desired, to return accountability to the urban denizens as much as rural folk.

In accordance with our belief that local governance works best, we acknowledge the ability of any new town to form with the consent of 75% of the people of an area where the population is greater than 500 people if unincorporated, or from an existing population if the size of the new town will be at least 2,500 people. The days when people get trapped under a city that does not work their local community will not continue.

The same logic applies for the county level government, which has no population restrictions, but has geographic limitations that are very important. New Albion has the goal of seeing every part of our country equally engaged from the rural to the urban areas, and as such, we have deliberately invested the legislative authority to reflect geographic diversity rather than population density, honoring our foundation in our blood and soil rather than in utility and idealism. As such, we have placed a minimal territorial requirement for new counties that they must be at least

200 square miles in territory. 98% of the land presently imagined in New Albion well exceeds this acreage, and we may grandfather in the few exceptions, but the reason this is so vital is because it prevents politics from becoming so disconnected ever again.

In the same way that new towns may form from existing cities or unoccupied territory, so too can new counties be made. If, across contiguous towns in an existing county, a petition to form a new county attracts 75% of the vote, then it shall be admitted with all the rights and responsibilities conveyed. A caveat is no county may be divided in two wherein both the mother county and the descendant are both not at least 200 square miles upon separation, and each has to have a population of at least 5,000 people. We put these caveats in because we want our counties to represent the people as well as the land.

For both towns and counties, any two or more bordering entities may also choose to merge should 75% of the people in all affected locales agree. Such consolidations must correspond to the population and size requirements as listed above.

New principalities may be created in just the same fashion as new towns or counties. The foundation of a new principality by the citizens requires the inclusion of at least five counties which possesses a population in excess of 250,000 people, and which garners the support of over 75% of the population in all the existing counties. Such restrictions are in place at this level because principalities are designed to be larger administrative districts, but if the people want, our kingdom is designed to have maximal flexibility within reasonable economic bonds.

Several exceptions exist. Non-contiguous islands already existing with a population over 100,000 as Prince Edward Island does may be admitted as a principality. Additionally, should future treaties define borders in a way that divides presently existing states outside New Albion, the Crown in consultation with the counties themselves being admitted and the neighboring states shall make the determination for the new lines to be adopted. As an example, if the three western counties of Maryland were to join New Albion as part of a mutually agreed upon treaty with the sovereignty entity of Maryland, they may be integrated into an existing neighbor state like Pennsylvania or West Virginia.

At this point, it is impossible to know what the map of the future will look like, but our determination remains fixed upon bringing those places in voluntarily who want to join us, working with neighbors to make intelligent borders driven by the nature of the land and concerns of the people as opposed to lines on the map. Lastly, we will provide the opportunity to begin realizing the transition now as we work diligently across counties to make this nation a reality.

The final level of governance is the kingdom as a whole. One monarch represents the whole of the New Albion people and represents an indivisible entity. Upon joining New Albion, any principalities admitted acknowledge the sovereignty of the Crown, and they are assumed to be integral and co-equal parts who are forever to remain thereafter part of our unified nation. We are not making all these efforts now to fight battles over secession later, so want to be very clear about what the expectations are. New Albion is not just a set of lands, but the birth of a new people who choose to realize and connect the best parts of Europe with a renewal of North American spirit.

The requirement for accession for external principalities into the Kingdom is the support of a majority of the people in a majority of the counties. You'll note this standard is much lower, and the reason is simple. We understand that in creating a new world that we need to take some leaps of faith, and we want people to work with us to realize this exciting new vision. We also will not allow big cities to veto the aspirations of rural folk, and in designing and implementing the first tenuous steps of this project, New Albion is learning how we must grow to succeed.

Since this is a monarchy, I will conclude with the titles of ranks from the civil side. Please remember this is a monarchy and aristocracy of merit, not heredity, so everyone who holds office has earned their role, and we aim for a most excellent civil administration.

Baron – The lowest noble rank is an unelected honorarium bestowed by either the King or a Prince for individuals of distinction in whom the state invests its appreciation and confidence.

Count – Selected by the mayors, the Count represents the lowest administrative level of nobility, but also has the most responsibilities including legislative, judicial, and enforcement functions.

Mark – The Mark is an administrative minister of the highest level in service to the Prince, and may be elevated by such.

Duke – The Duke is an administrative minister of the highest level in service to the King, and may be elevated by such.

Prince – The Prince is responsible for the defense and well-being of his principality with responsibilities akin to a governor as well as certain cultural responsibilities within the Crown.

King – The King is responsible for the defense and well-being of the realm and being the cultural leader of New Albion, assuming administrative oversight akin to a President.

It is envisioned that successful mayors will be chosen as Counts. From the ranks of former mayors and Counts the lesser nobility should be filled with the future Marks appointed by Princes and Dukes appointed by the King. The King shall select Princes. For every jurisdiction, the office holder must live in that district.

Counts may be removed by the mayors. Marks may be removed by the Princes. Dukes may be removed by the King. Either any Prince or the King may only be removed by a vote of 75% of the people in the relevant jurisdiction, or by specific measures listed later to represent the unanimous consent of other levels of government.

Princes are selected by the King and serve for life unless they resign or accede to become King. The King shall designate his successor in secret from amongst the Princes. No two Kings in succession shall come from the same principality or the same family (to the second cousin).

We lay out all these details because it is important for you to understand everyone from the highest to the low is held to account. The managers and administrators who we imagine as the center of our efforts are held to account by the Crown. The legislature is easily changeable by the people, through the mayors. Even the Crown, which exists to promote unity and collaboration is not beyond the reach of the people, and this is done because we do not want a civil war to be necessary if a ruler is appointed who fails in their duty. We think this works so much better, because it brings checks and balances back into the equation, and having laid out some details, let's go into each rank and office in more detail.

Chapter Seven: Town Governance

The community is the heart of governmental life in New Albion, where we expect most decisions to be made, where we want our people to be actively involved, and where we have deliberately invested the greatest taxing authority as testimony to such. To understand how this all works, the best way to describe this is to share a year in the civic calendar.

For those who aren't from New England, unless you are incredibly well read in history, you may have never heard of a Town Meeting before, but it is a central component of how our communities have functioned for several hundred years. Once per year, everyone in the community gathers to hear a presentation of the budget by either the elected or appointed leader. In New Albion, this component is simplified by having all communities have a Mayor to serve in that role as opposed to the current practice of allowing either a Select Board or surrogate like Town Manager to accomplish this role. The leader, whom we will call Mayor going forward, presents each line of the budget for public consideration and the opportunity is created to ask questions, amend the budget, and ultimately to pass or reject the budget line by line until a majority of those gathered agree to its adoption.

Upon adoption, that becomes the budget for the next calendar year, and whatever costs are proposed must reflect the budget. Policy becomes obvious as the expense accounting must be included, and historically, towns have had to keep surplus funds in reserve for unpredictable events. Much of what towns spend is related to infrastructure upkeep with water/sewer/roads, law enforcement and emergency services, some economic development, and code enforcement. It is reasonable to expect that will continue in New Albion, but one thing we do quite differently, and it is on purpose, is we don't formally list out the powers per level.

With the exception of certain prerogatives reserved to the Crown as inherent to national level governance, we actually want to see the different levels of government collaborating on projects of shared responsibility, permit local areas to act in areas which they think to their benefit, and move away from this idea that one form of government exists to fight a turf war over authority.

An important element of the Town Meeting and the one which always proves the most controversial will be the setting of the tax rate for the town. As you may recall, each of the four levels of government split 25% of the tax revenue from the national sales tax whose annual rate will be determined by the Accounting prior to these meetings. But, the town, if so chosen by the people themselves, can choose to elevate this rate to whatever they so select to pay for the projects contemplated in their budget. History suggests most places will select a marginal tax rate to encourage settlement and please residents, but there will be places that want to attempt a larger project from time to time, and may agree to pay an extra burden to realize their dream with their tax dollars. If that scares you, then all the better inducement to encourage civic participation and have a system where people engage.

Once this is resolved, the next duty of business will be to elect the Mayor. Any citizen who is a resident of the town will be eligible to serve, and the winner shall be decided by a first past the post election where all people over the age of 25 are eligible to run and vote. Any person who demonstrates their residency and who files intent papers to be eligible shall be on the ballot without needing to collect signatures or pay anything beyond a nominal administrative fee. We don't want parties in New Albion dividing us up in two, but we instead want the best men and women in our towns to step forward and lead their communities.

An election shall be held where there will be an opportunity for candidates to be heard in a public forum prior to the vote. We are not going to have campaign restrictions because we count on the people in our thousands of communities to do a better job of giving us a crop of strong and thoughtful leaders than the idea we can somehow find whomever has more money spent for marketing rules more wisely from far away.

It is an irony of this monarchy that we are probably more genuinely democratic than the existing system, but that's because we recognize the value of continuity from above and consensus from below, and in investing so much authority in the town and county, we have tried to make it hard for the people to see their autonomy so degraded once more.

The election will be held, and whomever wins will serve for the remainder of the calendar year. There are no term limits so you can keep voting for whomever you like as long as you like. Voting will be done by secret ballot, and any national issues such as recall petitions for the Crown, as well as accession or division of political units, will also happen at this time.

Once elected, the Mayor has several duties. He will be responsible for implementing the budget and developing the presentation for the next year. The Mayor shall be paid for his services in accordance with the budget approved by the people. He will also need to think about how to develop the economics of the town, what rules and regulations it will promote, and any special ordinances that are under consideration.

From the budgetary side, we want New Albion to be more concerned with wealth creation rather than debt servicing, so we are not going to allow any level of government to carry a debt load absent a declared emergency approved by higher levels. For too many years, government at every level has adopted this terrible habit of buying things today and sticking the cost on the next generation which politicians love because they don't have to pay the cost, just the debt servicing. However, as we sit in countries which now owe more than we make, seeing how that is inflating our currency and destroying our wealth, the time is finally upon us to get out of debt and stay that way, keeping a sound reserve and adopting a balanced role in developing towns.

If towns want to change what they are doing, we have deliberately left them the ability to adopt whatever depth of taxation they like, so long as they can persuade their public of the necessity of such action. But what we cannot permit is financing projects and running into debt. We realize this will make things take longer, but there will be opportunities for towns to work with other levels of government in cooperation, strengthening plans as collaboration without control creates best practices and encourages greater accountability. What it will also accomplish is a more predictable degree of cost stability across years, and help sustain a currency against inflation which is a worldwide calamity in the making.

We also want to allow towns to adopt whatever laws they see fit for how they want to live as long as they are in accordance with all above and the basic principles of New Albion. Such laws may be brought to the ballot by the people via referendum process for their town and will be discussed at the annual Town Meeting and voted upon during the Mayoral Election. The Mayor is also capable of putting such laws on the ballot directly for public consideration, and we envision that most laws that govern daily life in New Albion are going to come from this level. As much as the finances run through the Counties for the national level, the real opportunity for development is hyperlocal, and we are excited to see what innovations emerge. We also recognize many people just want a quiet life the way things have always been, and this system puts the power to accomplish just that in your capable hands.

This will take some time to sort out in practice, and we are deliberately not going into every choice that will be made between the levels of government, but one of the questions New Albioners need to shake out is precisely which functions we want to see conducted at what level. Although there are no restrictions, there are many times when it will make sense not to duplicate services, which is why I think we will see agencies like licensing and what not remain at the principal level. As envisioned, most of what happens at the higher levels involves either mass infrastructure projects that positively impact multiple communities, cultural developments designed to strengthen the nation, education investiture, military obligations, or agencies needed at the national level for interactions with external actors and to coordinate intergovernmental cooperation. This leaves a lot for communities to consider as their own obligation, and I think what we will find is different principalities will balance the three lower tiers of power differently, and we will see what works best.

Education is one area about which we should have a more in-depth discussion. The *Atlantic Charter* guarantees the right of parental choice about where their students and it is fully our intent to see each student have access to the best quality of education from the state as a necessary option. Historically, funding for the students have come from the most local level, but New Albion is going to change this system and shift the funding per pupil to the principal level, because we want to invest heavily in our future as our children regardless of the wealth or poverty of any community. That said, the reconciliation between towns and principalities will be that towns can invest in public infrastructure which will be used for public schooling, either by working individually or in unison as they choose, and any added investment will certainly be welcome.

It's worth taking a few moments to describe why a program dead set on decentralization everywhere else thinks differently on education funding, and the biggest reason is because education against our own interests has been the heart of the culture war tearing apart the West. The Crown of New Albion is charged with the high duty of defending the values of our nation, and we want schools to reflect a positive representation of our people, our history, our accomplishments, and our aspirations, and we want to invest our Princes with the duty to ensure our children learn those lessons instead of the cynical self-hatred we do today.

From the very inception of New Albion, we have consistently stated this desire to see the cultural sphere be the highest concern of the monarchy because we need this unity. Without it, we will fight again in just a generation, so while we welcome alternatives for parents to honor their lifestyles, we also want to redefine the cultural mainstream toward health, honor, and hope.

We see the future of our nation as a patchwork of little towns offering a nearly infinite variety of ways to approach the future.

Some places will want very little in way of goods and services, and others may try to rethink how government works entirely. It's exciting to imagine and this most accurately reflects the history of our land. I had the opportunity to visit so many of the first settlements over the years from Nova Scotia to Virginia, and what struck me was this commonality that small groups of people who knew one another were willing to take big changes to live a better life. Some prospered, many died, but they shared a determination that still rings true to us today.

Many will choose to be open. Others will choose to be insular. For Europeans seeking greater depth, for Native Americans who want to reclaim the old ways, and for minorities maybe looking to carve out their own slice in the Arboreal Kingdom, we have tried very hard to allow those different paths needed if we are to find not just peace, but prosperity and innovation in the interactions we adopt.

As someone who has spent the last five years living in towns whose population is under two thousand, I can share there is something healthy about knowing who is around you, and building a work of love together that meets your needs. While bigger budgets can buy more, they usually can't do more other than replace what exists or build infrastructure. We want you to build culture, to have unique towns, and to have every single town be vital. You have money to fix your community in New Albion, the authority to act, and the encouragement to see your hometown live onward. It's good to escape this idea we can't work where we live, and as will be profiled in the final book of the quartet, we really are thinking hard how to counter the model whereby everyone goes to the city. If our system is inefficient, how much freer shall we be, because we are not robots whose ingenuity will be prodded through conformity.

We trust our people to select wise mayors, keep them in line through approved budgets, and to see the mayors themselves work hard administering their towns. Much of this is an art rather than a science, so for as much as political scientists might prefer an itemized description of all that is involved, it is most accurate to say know your people, connect to them, and anticipate their needs while meeting their expectations.

Given the division of funds, the mayors will likely have to be diplomats. For as much as they can do on their own, they will have to work closely with the county and the Princes to get the best value for their people. Princes will be the very best of us chosen to help facilitate this, but as for the Counts, the unique thing is the mayors will be entirely responsible for that decision on their own.

Called upon to serve duty as an appeal board for the county courts, mayors get a taste of what the Counts deal with while getting to use their own judgment. Furthermore, they select who will serve as Count, who can be removed any time the Accounting is not in quarterly or special session by a majority vote for a replacement. Should the Count become deceased, such replacement will happen immediately for that person achieving the plurality of a vote of all mayors who will then be appointed to the higher office.

Our towns are our homes and in New Albion, the only limitations are those of budget and imagination. We want our people to live where they choose, because we believe in tradition and fidelity, not trying to make a system define who we are as frankly most sides do these days. It's a throwback, and the path to our survival.

Chapter Eight: County Governance

There are three primary functions for the Count, the appointed official by the mayors of his county, which are judicial, law enforcement, and legislative in function. Except for the King himself, this is likely the most important office in the land, and as such, we want to review why power is invested at precisely this level, and why we chose to unite certain function in a novel fashion.

In the current system, the county level government primarily handles issues related to legal issues and law enforcement. Economies of scale outside of all but the largest cities make it more logical to have these functions above the town level, and we have a very long tradition of sheriffs serving as the key police or peace officer, a term we want to restore, for the interests of the people. A sheriff, charged with serving warrants of the court, and historically having served as jailer in many cases, is basically the chief enforcement officer of the court and the defender of the law both for the citizens against one another and for the judicial function.

Although there was a lengthy digression into these duties in the sections on criminal and civil law, a quick review is New Albion has basically made the Count the sheriff, the judge, and the warden for his county. We recognize this is more than one person can handle which is why there will be deputies for law enforcement, arbiters of the courts, and wardens to administer the jail, but what matters is the recognition the Count is ultimately the face of accountability for all these actions, and that this person ultimately knowing how the good and the bad is going in his county, is also the best and most realistic way to develop sound national policy.

If you've ever talked to a sheriff, a warden, or most local judges, they realize the world far closer to the reality of what it is as opposed to our current legislature where people get paid to pass things without ever necessarily experiencing the impact of their decisions. We consider it reasonable to rely upon experience, and a keen appreciation of nature so honed, to serve as central to our system both for our people and as the foundation for making law.

For the role as judge, the Count will learn what issues impact his people, what crimes are a real problem, and see who is responsible. Where mayors have to work more through compromise, we want our Counts to learn proper exercise of strong authority and sentencing people to account for their actions teaches a lesson required for those who choose the path of service. This is not a role for everyone, and not for just who is most likable, but for those who can do it well and face the challenge of making hard choices.

This is one reason the Count is not elected. Mayors are going to be far more susceptible to political pressure, and also are going to represent a demanding audience who will be difficult to satisfy. It's not unfair to say this is a meatgrinder designed to produce the links we need to connect the top and the bottom, and we want to find truly talented officials to serve in our much smaller, but therefore needing to be much more capable, vision of civil service.

One of the most important duties the Count will need to manage is the hiring of capable surrogates. More than any other office, this level requires bringing in professionals to see the various functions are accomplished appropriately. With the legal system in particular, the case load could quickly become onerous without the appointment of excellent arbiters, and depending upon the size of the county, the Count likely will essentially rely heavily on those he brings in for such administrative purposes.

Court cases are complex, challenging, and time consuming. Given those problems, it is understandable why historical thinkers have chosen to separate these functions, and yet have we also not witnessed how judges have so often become a law unto themselves because of the authority so invested? The independent judiciary has frankly set itself above all other government as the ultimate arbiter, and having seen any number of questionable decisions upheld on the basis of their authority alone, New Albion has moved away from that model both by abandoning a national judiciary, but more importantly, by making our judges accountable and our legislators aware of what their laws and budgets are enacting.

The case load is probably beyond one person to manage in any but the least busy county, so developing this system through the arbiters will be essential, as will be the quick administration of justice. Although such design might appear a flaw, one thing we hope this causes is swifter application of justice, and even more effort to avoid turning people into criminals lest time be wasted. Every society will have those who cause mischief, but needs to work constantly to make sure reasonable discontent can find better avenues of expression and see that we only devote our incarceration efforts to those most threatening.

One thing the Count cannot delegate is his responsibility for sentencing. For criminal trials especially, he will have to enact and impose whatever sentencing the people request. Deliberately, this has been left open to reflect differences in how the public may want to see crime tackled by area. He may promulgate a basic guideline for usage to save time, but must inflict the sentence himself. And there will be no parole boards – sentencing is what is enacted.

For the role as sheriff, the Count will be called upon and expected to ensure the rights and responsibilities of the people are upheld, their liberties are protected, and their safety secured. Our primary law enforcement function is being deliberately left to this level with the assumption that Sheriffs have authority above local Law Enforcement, and we do this to protect the integrity of county governance. Consider for a moment that New York has a Police Department whose budget is greater than some militaries, and perhaps you might better understand why we want law enforcement to be more diffuse.

On a daily basis, this will mean providing support to communities, arresting criminals and basic law enforcement of the code included in Chapter Four. We also are hoping to develop a new rapport between those who enforce the laws and the populace at large, and that's why we're trusting most functions from higher levels to the sheriffs as well. We have seen the incredible malfeasance of the FBI and other agencies, and there may be no greater threat to the people than the accumulation of such power with legal authority at the highest level, and so we're going to heavily diminish that presence.

For the role as warden, county prisons will replace these cynical operations of private detention facilities. We do not want incarceration to become a growth industry as it has sadly done in America, and we want to keep our people out of jail. There are far too many state and federal overreaches where we just dump our people, and with the exception of military facilities, this level will be our sole prison allotment. If counties so choose, there is no issue with combining resources for one facility and sharing responsibility for such on a financially equitable basis. But that choice is reserved to the counties.

Additionally, it is reasonable that county prisoners may be used as labor in service while incarcerated so long as these jobs are no different than others might work in the private or public sector. Counts may decide for themselves in conjunction with the warden how much they want to invest in rehabilitation versus other criteria, but within the basic rights protected for New Albion, the idea that we cannot make use of these people is discarded.

Having covered all that, we can finally talk about the Accounting which is the legislature or parliament of New Albion. It consists of all Counts in office, and has the authority to pass the national budget developed by the Crown, set the national tax rate, and to declare war. There will be no permanent building constructed for this purpose, nor will there be a permanent capital, because we do not want a permanent bureaucracy to cluster in one place. Instead, the capital will move quarterly, with participation in person or remotely permitted, with the caveat that every Count must attend at least one of the four annual meetings in person.

Most laws are restricted to passage at the community level, but only the Accounting can amend the *Atlantic Charter*. If a suggested right or responsibility is to be added, it must pass with a 75% majority in the Accounting, and then be confirmed by 75% of the public by referendum in the next election. We do not want to make it easy to change the rules, but we do not want it to be impossible either.

For policies and procedures, it is anticipated that the higher ranks of administrative nobility will constantly be working to develop best practices in consultation with the Counts both to assess the public need, but also to ensure their budgets will be approved. In the same way the Town Meeting does, the ultimate budget must be approved by the Accounting, and although the budget will be annual, the quarterly meetings are designed to work through the various issues and create greater understanding.

A restriction upon the Accounting is they cannot contemplate an imbalanced budget, except in times of declared war. They are instructed to run a surplus, preserve where they can, and think of the concerns of tomorrow with equal vigor as the concerns of this day. As well as any rank in our government, we believe they will have their pulse on the needs of the nation, and so we entrust this task to their wisdom leaving the towns to explore autonomous paths and the Crown to unite and defend the people.

Heavily involved with the responsibilities of the Count is considering the finances of the realm. While the Count retains one quarter of revenue coming into the nation primarily for its judicial and law enforcement duties, it also sets the rates for what everyone will get in a given year. As much as the Crown will present its budget for the national government, and the Princes will consult as well, they do not have fiscal authority to independently raise their own revenue from taxation, and so they must work to reconcile all branches of government over the course of the year.

Furthermore, any new source of derived revenue must also receive approval from the Accounting, who will then be charged with making assessments about the validity of such projections as a deliberative body. It is expected most information will be provided by the Marks and Dukes to answer inquiry, and best practice would see the annual budget be a deliberation considered year-round so that issues of conflict can be addressed in advance. But these other revenues such as income taxes, tariffs, user fees, and foreign visitor differentials are within the purview of the Counts.

In terms of orientation, the design of New Albion is supposed to encourage money to accumulate more readily at the more local level rather than the national, but what we also hope to accomplish is to see a taxation apparatus which also favors the small over the big. These issues will be contested each year, but our deliberate starting point is we want to tax the income with a sliding scale designed to help local businesses against huge conglomerates, and with geographic restrictions trying to encourage regional actors rather than corporate affiliates. The Counts should be very sympathetic to these measures, and we expect they will do well.

A challenge of the Accounting is it may become quite large. If we were only to take the states of Maine, New Hampshire, and Vermont, we would have a sum of 42 counties. But as we expand, this number could easily exceed 1,000, which will be a challenge. Yet, in the same way we want decentralized governance, and we recognize it will be able to do less as the Accounting grows, this itself constitutes another check and balance. A small kingdom of three states will necessarily need to coordinate more because of greater susceptibility to foreign threats, and so we would want a more active Accounting. Conversely, if we occupy the northern half of North America and the two thousand plus counties that requires, we're going to need to be highly decentralized.

The Accounting is not Congress or the Commons. This is not a place for posturing and long debates in dispute. We want to emphasize unity for the nation, collaboration in vision, and autonomy locally for moth things. As such, we will not be having a ton of meetings, but instead will leave those actions to the bureaucracy, itself made up of people who were former Counts, and to whom we trust the welfare of this new nation. One could be skeptical of such a choice, but we feel like giving control over the money to chunks of the land itself is going to work so much better in terms of seeing healthier distribution and greater accountability.

Taking a big step back, the goal of New Albion is promotion of the best over what most might say they want. We structure our government to realize these principles and the Counts are the way we identify our very best people through their service while held account to the citizenry at large so that we know who is capable to lead us all in the future. Where former times have used either money or bloodlines, two things which still frankly dominate the world today, we wanted to create something better here where we found a standard by which we could measure our most devoted servants against one another.

We also have an excellent historical precedent for how this structure will work in how the Senate functioned in the United States before passage of the 17th Amendment which required direct elections. Today Senators have become largely partisan hacks, but they used to be principled representatives for their state governments. In that same vein, Counts are the representatives of all our communities, accountable to them, and linked deeply to a particular place of land rather than a set of conflicting interests. We hope that deep bond serves to disable partisanship, and offer opportunities for new cooperation as every person, even a city dweller, has to be a localist in New Albion.

Given the scope of responsibilities already listed for the County, we envision those functions beyond the judicial, enforcement, and legislative functions will be mostly yielded to the towns, with a few efforts being managed at the principal level. As justice for the land and being the voice of the people are highly important, we trust our Counts to be the eyes and ears of our new nation.

The one exemption is there will be a county level militia that exists under the authority of the Count for activation in times of war or emergency. Chapter Twelve will cover this in much further detail.

Chapter Nine: Principal Governance

Principal Government in New Albion represents what is currently State level in the United States or Provincial level in Canada. We will discuss two ranks here which are the Princes, who essentially serve a similar function as Governors or Premiers, and Marks who serve as the chief Deputies or Ministers.

In New Albion, since we have devolved power to lower levels, the Principality plays a somewhat different role than we see in the current systems. Our higher ranks are primarily concerned with developing the culture and people's quality of life, so what the Princes and Crown actually do is step in to fulfill those functions which must be handled at higher levels due to economy of scale and beyond that serve as promoters and administrators for the efforts to develop the nation.

In terms of responsibilities, it is believed that Princes will be responsible for developing the education system, the culture of the province, infrastructure between towns, and health care networks. All of these represent investments beyond the capacity of towns to handle on their own, but are areas essential to the long-term wellness and vitality of the nation.

Let's discuss education first. As precursor to this discussion, recall that every parent has the opportunity to remove their children from state education as a guaranteed right, but we have learned from the massive mistake made in America it is not enough to decentralize education, because then you allow others with questionable motives to take control over your children, and through them the ideas of generations to follow. To preserve our culture, we must be intimately involved with sculpting education.

Now, the third book will go into exhaustive detail on this question, but as preview for that work, what we are thinking is an entirely new approach toward education. We want to embrace a whole person concept that is deeply rooted in our European traditions, and expands beyond a basic curriculum to deliver hands on experience for valuable life skills, trades that can be used for employment, and higher standards across the board.

The particulars are still under discussion, but key goals we want to achieve is to expose our pupils to the details of European culture in all its variations, of New Albion culture as the unity of such, and to include the best of American and Canadian traditions as what we hold as our proud inheritance. We will emphasize teaching critical thought, remove all political correctness from the curriculum, and seek to foster a culture of success for all students by managing the efforts at the state level versus the local.

In America, we realize that people often moved to high rent districts and agreed to pay a higher tax burden specifically for better schools. We want people to realize our goal here is not to have students be moved from their neighborhoods to access better schools, but to bring accountability to those schools which have failed because of low expectations, a subpar criterion, and the influence of political factors. We will work to liberate teachers from mediocrity, and replace those who are unable to elevate their game.

Things we do differently are we want to ensure every graduating student has not just a deep foundation of knowledge, but real-life skills such as gardening, cooking, mechanical ability, shooting, and a specific trade they can carry with them all their lives. Independence comes from knowing one can survive many different situations, and where our system to know has emphasized specialization against a broader based approach, we are returning the confidence and authority to our young people to know they can do anything. Between better academic processes and the revitalization of the family, we believe there is every reason to be much more confident that our young people will be achievers.

In a similar vein, since the primary funding source of the universities continues to be the state, our Princes will be taking charge of all but a few special Crown universities for specific statecraft roles. We are ending the sorry situation of requiring our young folk to go into absurd levels of debt by reducing tuition unilaterally, increasing standards, and recognizing we don't need a society where everyone goes to college. New Albion has long contemplated a general jubilee on that debt as a national refund, and we do not want to see our young people mortgage their future to develop their present in the future as they are forced to do today.

The goal is to see our higher education system serve the interests of our people, filling needs in our society while permitting the search for knowledge to find honest application. We honor such exploration while recognizing there are many paths to success in New Albion, and a rethink of the entire university system is one that will become a national conversation upon inception. What we know we do not want is to put the burdens upon our young people as they are just beginning in life, that we will not permit these academics to teach self-hatred and call it progress, and that we need not submit to their control just because it has been done this way before. We must do better, and we shall.

The intersection between culture and education is much more explicit in New Albion because we are working to develop an informal framework that is entirely new called the Kindred System. What we propose to do is create cultural events and networks based upon ethnic interests that also represent networks which people can join throughout their lives to find comfort, inspiration, opportunity, skills, and belonging. These will develop organically but offer an alternate means of organization that are designed to catalyze creativity and connection to accelerate our unification.

Our current culture is so isolating and alienating between all the masks people are forced to wear, how we twist ourselves to service the needs of capital, and how technology is dividing us from one another with frightful rapidity. To combat this and bring people back together, we look not just to localizing government to solve issues, but to crafting larger cultural networks as patrons. Specifically, if you are English, French, German, or any other European identity, we want to help you explore and integrate with your heritage in a real way no longer encouraged today. Although our primary emphasis is upon European culture, we also have variants for those who come from Native or other stock, because we think happiness comes from knowing who you are, and that is not a disconnected individual, but instead a chain in a long line of ancestors going back many years, whatever your ancestry.

In his capacity as Prince, and in parallel with the King, you will see considerable investment of time and energy, hopefully in concert with a reborn civil society, to push these ideas and those which beautify and glorify our culture. We believe tomorrow can be better, and the core of this project is the reclamation of the West as a project of a nobler vision.

Nationalists understand a nation is the people, not the cold austerities of a disconnected state. We want our folk to know themselves, to celebrate the passage of seasons, and connect across generations. As such, much of what the Prince does is a form of artistry, designed to cultivate the gardens of the mind and spirit in his realm, and to use his budget beyond the expressed obligations above to bolster and connect excellent efforts toward fruition.

As such, he will be given sanction to appoint people within his realm who have shown distinction to serve as Marks. It is anticipated these people will come from the ranks of the former mayors and Counts, although for certain projects, it may very well make sense to appoint private citizens who come from entrepreneurial or other professional backgrounds. But what we want is a well-developed bureaucracy whose primary task will be to develop and execute projects as funded by the Accounting. This will require collaboration and planning in advance, but we believe this system which requires feedback along the line will work well.

When we look at the expectations for a smart and active people, we cannot help but consider the question of health care. The rights and responsibilities of the *Atlantic Charter* inform us that we need to preserve choice and bodily sovereignty while honoring our commitment to the health of the nation. As such, we anticipate and endorse having access to the highest quality health care system whereby use of this is made available to all citizens. The complex nature of the calculations involved is such that much thought will have to be put into how this will precisely work, but as putting our people's well-being first is something we consider non-negotiable, New Albion will do whatever is required to make sure all basic needs are covered while we try to offer the best options for more complicated cases.

Rather than trying to offer a ready-made solution for this important challenge, we assert all options are on the table. We will consider both private and public alternatives with hybrid approaches, and will be unafraid to use government intervention to control costs. An idea we have is we want to encourage health tourism, using visitors to experience what we intend to be the best and most innovative health care in world, to help sustain the costs of looking at what we can do that is new while we work to ensure that basic level treatment is held at a very sustainable cost. What we absolutely must do is ensure that we do not hide behind excuses for failing to sustain the health of our people.

Given the improved education and use of reason rather than marketing based propaganda, we hope to greatly assist this task by working to see our people have access to healthier food, face less unhealthy contamination in our environment, and we will encourage both our educational institutions and our governmental agencies to work together to tell us what is really happening and what impact both technology and the environment have on nutrition, agriculture, the public health, and climate projections.

Within New Albion, many are concerned about these issues. Others are highly skeptical because of a lack of trust of the sources and intentions of such research. As such, we need our own independent evaluations, and we want to move past this self-defeating tendency where the only research that gets funded is that which delivers the most sensational findings. We'll take truth instead, good or bad, and build our plans on that foundation.

The other big projects which will likely fall to the Principality are questions of licensing and infrastructure. It would be inefficient to try to have so many different licensing agencies to return these authorities to the town or county, so for areas where public safety is a legitimate concern as with driving, we will continue to handle permitting at this level. We will work to streamline these functions, however, and ensure higher quality service.

The succeeding chapter is going to go into far greater detail about major infrastructure works and policy that the Crown will embark upon, but there is plenty that will be done by the Principalities and in conjunction with both higher and lower government. What we want to see emerge is a world class transportation system, which includes light rail, aviation, and more efficient automobiles. We want transportation to be easy, affordable, and to bring life to our small towns and cities alike, and especially as we erase the border between Canada and the United States, we hope to see new energy and communities develop in this to be opened space.

We are deliberately removing all these layers of bureaucracy that served to make it so impossible to begin projects as we want to spend less money talking and more money doing. Obviously, we will act responsibly with a mind toward environmental impact, but so often, the nature of projects is they basically become payoffs for people who needed to be bought politically. In New Albion, since the Princes are unelected, we don't have this requirement: We can simply serve the people, and you keep your check on our planning through the Accounting.

The Prince will be responsible, in conjunction with the Marks, and in consultation with the Accounting for financial reasons, for essentially offering the master plan of how to connect towns, bolstering the people of his realm, and managing those levels of bureaucracy which naturally rise to this level. It is anticipated that some of these costs may exceed the quarter sales tax return, and so we will see other measures and funds devoted to ensuring the viability of these essential services such as user fees and licensure.

As such, we realize each principal government may look quite different from one another, and we welcome this devolution. What works well in Quebec probably will not be as appropriate in Ohio, and the genius of federalism when well designed is to recognize that one solution doesn't fit all because our cultural expectations vary, our economies are as divergent as our climates, and we know that our people want to live their lives in accordance with their local traditions. While we want to forge a common culture, we recognize that the most meaningful parts will always be local, dynamic, and distinctive, so we preserve these possibilities through allowing a wide degree of latitudes.

Princes shall be selected by the King from amongst those who have a demonstrated track record of excellence, are recognized as leading citizens of the principality in question, and whose service to the people is beyond doubt. The Prince may serve a lifetime role, although it is expected and encouraged that retirement be undertaken should they feel unequal to the role, and the suggestions of the outgoing servant shall be taken in deep consideration in the new Prince to be appointed. Retirees who served at least ten years in honorable service of any rank shall be permitted to maintain their earned rank as an honorific.

The check and balance is the people have the right to remove the Prince with a 75% removal vote in any given year. The process by which this will be conducted is as follows: Each year, the Princes and King shall receive a nonbinding vote of confidence from the people as part of the annual election. In any year in which any officer receives a rating where more than two-thirds of the people disapprove of the job they are doing, the next election shall feature a ballot whereby a recall will be considered.

Should any Prince be removed by this method, the King shall appoint his replacement. This system is not designed to disrupt the flow of leadership, which is nonpartisan, but rather recognizes that occasionally events may warrant action. By the same standard, the King and the Accounting can, in tandem, remove a Prince with 3/4 vote from power for national security.

The next thing that we must consider is the Princes are the pool from which the next King shall be chosen. Although we used the standard masculine as the neuter form, there is no prohibition in New Albion about the appointment of a person of either sex to any office in the land. So, the relevant ranks are Baroness, Countess, Marquess, Duchess, Princess, and Queen, in conversion. These people will be the future of our nation, so let us pray they guide us well and that they become the excellent servants we require.

Instead of having a system focused on competing ideas, we have striven hard to build our foundation on collaboration, and we trust that our principalities will offer greater autonomy, greater success, and greater satisfaction than the existing system.

Lastly, the Princes have certain military requirements in terms of being able to muster the County militias, with the expectation that each Principality will host a Division or other assets and provide support for the basic infrastructure as such in conjunction with the Crown.

Chapter Ten: Kingdom Governance

The King is the very embodiment of New Albion, and he is presumed to speak with one voice for the whole of our nation. The Crown bears responsibility for many roles including those national functions you would expect like statecraft, war, the treasury, immigration, and borders. More importantly than these, however, is the responsibility to unite the people and work constantly toward forging greater links between our folk to become a single nation.

For civilian agencies, the King shall promote Dukes who will manage major projects, with military responsibilities reserved to officers according to their ranks. Dukes serve solely at the pleasure of the King and can be removed for any reason.

Consider the American or Canadian examples where we see our countries tearing apart at the seams because of ideological, ethnological, or economic divisions that better politics and a healthy culture would have overcome decades ago. New Albion, being the solution to this problem, will emphatically work to ensure we become one people when it comes to defending our beautiful home and the civilization which we must rekindle.

The King has the responsibility for the conduct of all wars. A declaration must be provided by the Accounting, although the King is permitted the right to imminent self-defense of the realm in case of attack. The Crown brings a request to the Accounting, and then the deliberation is considered with a simple majority enough for the declaration to be pronounced.

The King also has the right to craft and sign treaties which will require the ratification of the Accounting with a simple majority.

The Crown shall maintain a permanent core of diplomats and provide for embassies in all nations in accordance with international practice. It will also commission a school specifically for the conduct of such operations. It is expected that the Crown will also have the capacity to conduct information gathering activities as part of these actions which will be strictly limited to international figures.

A short digression is necessary here because most people who have been paying attention know the Central Intelligence Agency regularly violates such a mandate. Our espionage capacities are going to much more circumscribed, far less well funded, and we are deliberately avoiding building the whole bloated military industrial and federal law enforcement complex around it that so engulfed DC. Such problems are inevitable to any government, but we've worked hard to constrain this, not the least of which by following the original suggestion of the Constitution in spirit by not having a large standing army.

The Crown will maintain an Admiralty responsible for the protection of our coasts, sea, lakes, and rivers, and to produce and man ships for the accomplishment of such ends, as well as for the protection of our commerce. The security of the seaports shall be delegated to the Admiralty.   A Naval Academy shall be maintained

The Crown will also maintain the Military which will assume responsibility for both border security, as well as providing a rapid reaction force, and keep a permanent officer corps as advisor to the King and to train and advise local militias. A Military Academy shall be maintained.

It is no accident that we are returning authority over ports and borders to our military. New Albion was founded with three goals in mind: The security of our borders, the ability to control who enters, and the revitalization of our culture. As such, we satisfy two of our three key criteria by militarizing the borders, and we are depoliticizing the question of who enters and giving our men and women the ability to repel any invasion and contest any threat.

As is only sensible, immigration is specifically the province of the King's authority and an agency shall be established to determine the viability of all those who seek to enter New Albion. For a period to be determined upon inception of no fewer than three years, there will be a right of return for any American or Canadian to New Albion, whether they live within or without the borders, to be admitted as a fully qualified citizen. The Crown may make additional proclamations in consultation with the counties at the point of inception to recognize others as having a special right of return such as the Boer descendants of South Africa, as well as people in certain European countries.

For the future, what will happen is the Crown maintains unilateral discretion over who may enter the nation, but any refugees entering the country may only be settled in Counties where they are wanted as expressed by the local Count. We will quite explicitly be working to strengthen the uniquely European character of our homeland, although exceptions may be considered, so our goal is to return to first as an 85/15 split, and then to stabilize at 90/10. Exceptional outsiders may seek entry, but the determination of entry will be based on skill, desirability, cultural conformity, and the value of the entrant to New Albion, with zero presumed requirement we take anyone beyond those who are listed above. We will also consider families as a single unit.

For many years, people have been unwilling and unable to describe the real consequences of a culture that divides along racial lines, but New Albion is being honest about the issue instead. The reason America has been lost is we brought too many people in who thought differently than the outgoing majority had done, which made sense given how they are biologically adaptive to entirely different environments, and when that was coupled with a society that stopped assimilating people and instead encouraged the cancer that is multiculturalism, diversity to that degree destroyed the unity of the United States. The lesson and admonition to the future is that people are not interchangeable to an infinite degree, so while we may choose to incorporate a select few unlike us, we must constantly maintain and secure a majority for European folk should we want our values of reason, nature, grace, and loyalty to maintain. It has been tried many times to use ideas to overcome biology, and such wishes have only failed and led to the death and destruction of empires and peoples alike. This is why we also realize and warn our Canadian neighbors to join with us before your country is lost even more quickly for the same reason. We wish to live in love and harmony with those unlike us, with whom we will likely share a border one day, but in recognition of our differences and the requirement we have our own dedicated homeland to ensure our survival.

The Crown shall be responsible for the collection of all taxes and their distribution in accordance with the local laws. The Treasury does not ever possess such wealth beyond the Crown's quarter, but rather ensures the means by which transfer happens is instantaneous to the government in question. The Treasury reserves the right to print currency, and is expressly forbidden from contracting any central bank exterior to the government to handle the financial authority of New Albion.

Other duties which would be natural to the national level of government can be also assumed to apply, although we're looking to shrink the involvement of the national government in many areas. We do not contemplate major law enforcement resources, regulatory agencies which we reserved to the principalities, or the excessive overreach which so clouded America.

What the King will be doing is working to craft Great Projects and develop our culture and values. A unique assembly that will meet regularly and have offices throughout the land is the Royal Court of Barons. A collection of thinkers, scholars, and achievers, we want our best citizens to explore the potential for what we might accomplish, and the Crown may offer honorariums to our exemplars to create new ideas, artistry, or conceive projects for the good of our people.

With assistance from all lower levels of government, we see this manifest first as investments to revitalize culture. We love arts, music, gardens, theater, and want to promote familiarity with both our national languages of English and French throughout the land. We will seek to create a better and more uplifting alternative to what the media currently pushes, and use the power of social influence to help our people remember themselves and that we are truly an excellent folk capable of goodness as well as greatness.

Beyond this, the King will use such revenue as required to conduct those great projects that can unite the land. One example we have long contemplated is building upon our existing capacity in Quebec, Niagara, and Manitoba to become a fully self-sufficient hydro super power by building a tidal engine on the Bay of Fundy that would be able to power the whole of our nation, sell power to our neighbors, and potentially connect Nova Scotia directly to Maine to develop our eastern shore. We save the environment, link our people, and the beneficiaries will be the people not just in economic costs of cheaper energy, but in how we want you to get a dividend from this investment much as Alaska does with oil revenues.

The reality is the near future will see many jobs lost to automation, and while we are working swiftly to imagine and design an artisan based economy that is local, redundant, and resilient while allowing for a healthy level of innovation, there are problems coming down the line. The suggestion that universal basic income, or free welfare for all, will solve this will only cause hyperinflation and collapse, trends which will soon become apparent. Instead of that cynical approach, New Albion looks to build public infrastructure, especially in energy and health servicing, and use a portion of those proceeds to make clear Crown investments will offer shared benefit to all our people, with the division being between the Crown, the local governments, the local people, and the people at large. The specifics will depend upon the project, but we want to conceive of this government as your government, and to use our prosperity to directly improve the quality of our people.

While we hope to interact with the world, the reality is we may need to be a closed shop for a while. I say this because of ideological conflicts, ethnic animosities, the corrosive and widespread influence of international banking, and the many unknown factors we cannot predict. Our King should do his best to ensure New Albion always has the capacity to exist independently, and our people must remember this project we propose runs against the course of history which has long preferred submission and despotism, even in our own past. We will always have to be vigilant, and we must remember our sovereignty is preserved through the will and strength of our people to be expressed through unity and fidelity to each other and this wondrous land.

As your author and the person putting the most energy into imagining this project, I have claimed the title of Regent for New Albion to provide leadership and vision until such time as it may be enacted with the unanimous and joyful consent of we dissenters who dare to imagine something better in a most cynical time. I share this because my role is to help shepherd New Albion into existence until such time as we can see a gathering of counties who can choose their first King, whomever they may select, and then it will be the responsibility of future monarchs to maintain the line of succession. Uniquely, like with every other office, the Kingship is not hereditary, but must be bestowed to a succession whose requirements is they must be 25 years of age, a citizen of New Albion, and hail from a different Principality than the departing monarch. We must choose the very best person, who has vision appropriate for the time, and can create the love of our people.

Perhaps as a medievalist who has spent many years gaining an understanding of what monarchy truly represents, now is the time to explain in further depth why this has to be the system we choose as nationalists because many other voices will cry out for the apparently greater choices of republics or democracies. While those systems provide more chances for people to opine, the weakness of both is they create massive disunity and factionalism as people are readily split into parties who fight bitter wars that harden into systems trying to destroy one another with people just serving as lemmings for these ends. Consider either of our host countries as example, or anywhere else around the world. Democracy and republics rely upon systems which might value persons, but care little for people. Monarchy, by contrast, is a personal system built upon loyalty and the pledge of honor from the leader to serve the people and the people to endorse the leader. Such loyalty is sorely necessary in such a confusing world.

Furthermore, history has shown while democracies succeed in small communities where people can cooperate and the ability of corruption to overwhelm the system is low, which is why we preserve that benefit in its rawest form with mayors and town meetings, it does not convert upward to anything more than a cynical oligarchy that purchases people and governments alike. The republic worked admirably to settle the lands of this continent for our civilization, encouraging us into the wilderness, allowing the overcoming of tribal challenges, and reaching the extent of what geography would allow. But now, as a mature civilization, we are not the first sentries on the border, but a people which must either select if we will either try to maintain this empire to our own destruction into a million fragments, or if we have the courage to wrest the heart of what was the North American project into a new beginning that opens a new chapter.

Our King must be a storyteller, and though the details will change to reflect the challenges of the time, the fairy tale we require is about the victory of our people achieved through the fulfillment of our unique and irreplaceable talents. There is no magic formula by which this may be accomplished, save perhaps to ask to heaven above with faith that such a leader may occur in all times, and to work to create a society and systems that may create many such men and women to ensure that we endure and prosper.

One can claim such a person can have too much power, or that such imagination is too terrifying for the world to consider, but as nationalists, do we not see the extinction of so much we hold dear as impetus to finally act, and to do something well? A King may do much, far more than most men, but you have the ability to hold this one person to account so much more ably than these systems of shadow and deceit which darken our honest people with their clever lies. A kingdom requires courage and decency, which is precisely what we need to recover.

Should a future king prove unequal to the task, we've left means by which the public can force an abdication. This is a terrible and destructive power to reserve, which is why we've stuck to the 75% standard because removing a head of state is not meant to be a partisan tactic as it has so often become. The King is meant to serve all people, and discord will result, but we also recognize madness has come upon people from time to time, and that we reserve to the people the ability to remove the King by either such a vote or by the unanimous vote of the Princes. Should such a situation happen, the Accounting shall appoint the successor.

Let us pray that never proves necessary, and we close this examination of the structures and personnel of our government by reminding the King that his job is to serve the people, to harness the elites to their benefit rather than to exist as a class apart, to push a culture of truth and beauty, and to see the restoration of faith in ourselves and in goodness against the many evils which threaten us. Much discretion is left to this person to find, follow, and fix the problems which none other can address, and therefore, we must pray that all those who inherit this sacred duty are equal to the role.

As a final suggestion, just as the pope surrenders his surname upon acceding to the pontificate, the King of New Albion shall bear the name Albion as reminder he speaks for us all now. God Save the King and God Save New Albion!

Chapter Eleven: Taxes and Finance in Detail

Although less exciting than imagining a new government structure, it is as important to fully explain taxation and currency. This chapter will offer first thoughts on how the system could work, fully anticipating that we will have to adjust in practice. We have applied the **FLASH** strategy we promoted at the onset for questions of law to our financial system writ large. We seek a system which allows for government spending and taxation to be local, friendly and open with simplicity, honesty and accountability. However, to further improve the efficiency of the system and to remove the need for layers of bureaucracy, we're going to ask our people to think of money, taxes, and identification differently.

New Albion would like to have a single card that serves as identification, debit card, and tax ID. In America, given the many agencies which trace our data, such a proclamation could legitimately cause a panic, but we're actually trying to simplify how these three functions work and cut out many of those dreaded three letter agencies. Let's talk about why.

One of the most absurd stances of American politics for many years has been that it is a form of prejudice to require people to present valid photo identification when voting. This idea is promoted by people who want to push fraud and theft against the voting process. We want clear identification that makes evident the citizenship status, current residence, and identity of a person. Only those who show identification should be permitted to vote, and we intend this card to serve this purpose.

Furthermore, we are working to escape the traps of the banking system, and so many of these evolve out of complicated relationships between finance, accounting, and the state. States worry that people will cheat on their taxes, which they most certainly do, and citizens resent the encroachment of the state to collect such. The conflict rises to the point where authority to investigate, incarcerate, and even get into fire fights is assumed by the state to fund itself, and this relationship only gets uglier from there, as the Internal Revenue Code of the United States suggests.

If we are willing to extend a little trust in this new state, we can eliminate so much of that. Each citizen will have a card that serves both as ID and debit device, and it will automatically account and transfer the appropriate amount of sales tax and/or fees assessed for foreigners to the Crown servers which will then return the appropriate cost for the transaction. No accountants. No cheating. No drama. An honest society deserves an honest accounting, and I am utterly certain that the billions we will save by recording all transactions this way will represent a sea change that will make costs cheaper, businesses more competitive, and also limit the access to your private information.

We deliberately decided to constrain the ability to collect either wage or land taxes as a good faith demonstration of our respect for the privacy of our people, but also sound policy in regard to seeing a nation which has freer people. In exchange, we want to have a single card, never to be appended to your body, that has access to data needed, but where you maintain the key to unlocking all those records, because we want you to control your information. As we grow into this new economy, the thought is having that decentralized control will prove an immense asset to privacy, but it will also create efficiency that is vital to how we conduct commerce.

To put the idea into focus, let's consider how a transaction will work. If you want to buy a candy bar in your town, you would simply select the chocolate and bring it to the register as you do now. The price of the bar would already have been listed with a sign making clear the sales tax in the community in question. Your card would be inserted, and you would pay the listed cost plus the sales tax, have that amount deducted from your account with the funds immediately transferred to the vendor for the candy bar and the Crown for the taxes. Then, you go about your way.

Let's pretend the sales tax was twenty percent, which represents ten percent for the government at large, and another ten percent applied specifically to the community as having been approved at Town Meeting to fund a new gymnasium. What will happen is the Crown will retain 2.5 cents, the Principality collects 2.5 cents, the County gets 2.5 cents, and 12.5 cents will return to the Town.

For purposes of competition, the sales tax paid will depend upon the location of the sale for all point of sale purchases, with digital delivery-based purchases being dependent on the location of the delivery. Local communities have lost so much of their revenue from remote retailers, and we aim to restore these funds to the community and to ensure that taxation faced by brick and mortar retailers is now cost competitive with digital distribution. We want lively small towns and ownership.

Such information being available to the government for everyone who lives in a community, we have the capacity to remove all names from the aggregate data, which we would, and look at towns at a glance as well as counties, principalities, and the kingdom to accurately project a budget based upon popular expenditure, and to remove questions of false projection and waste by compilation of this data in easy to understand forms that will be available publicly for consideration by each level on an annual basis.

We are really deep in the weeds here, but the reason is because this is where theft and corruption happens, so the same way we expect the Accounting to make clear the national budget and the mayor to allow you to choose your town budget at the meeting, we want you to be empowered with honest data to make good decisions.

Before we leave the question of this data card, we want to make sure it has protections against identity theft which will be aligned with best practices, and will contemplate its use for other key information like licensure and health insurance, hoping the simplicity and uniformity represents a massive cost savings all around. Any time redundancy can be decreased in bureaucracy, that represents a real savings for the people.

I know some people are very fond of paper cash, so we want to explain we removed that because of how inefficient it is, and not because we hope to compel submission to some system. As our laws require, you have privacy, the ability to barter, and whatever else you like, but we needed to get into the corruption not just for people, but in using this same system in a modified format for purchasing and businesses as well, who are subject to a modified tax code.

The particulars of what user fees, income tax, tariffs, and other costs are incurred in a given transaction will be set up by the

Accounting, but all these individual transactions allow us to see in one clear glimpse how much revenue a company makes and how many losses they took or how much was invested in infrastructure or fixed assets. Instead of relying upon self-reporting, we can now see what actually happens, and assess a simple tax code without exemptions for business. The scales will be public, and as has been hinted at elsewhere, we're going to slide the taxation to be most heavy upon the highest earners. We want a society where wealth and ownership are distributed, and we intend on preventing the sort of monopoly effects that have been so corrosive to both liberty and opportunity.

Let's talk about the different taxes as classes and offer first thoughts on levels and costs. Since the sales tax is the basic cost of the land, there are two factors that will determine the rate. Firstly, both the Accounting at the national level and the town at the local level will have the capacity to exempt certain items from taxation. I know many towns and states have traditionally exempted food from such taxation as but one example. New Albion may elect to do the same, and the rate of the taxation depends specifically upon which items are exempted, and also which excise or luxury taxes may be enacted.

Only the Accounting will be able to implement these taxes by class, and the reason for this is largely we want to try to measure these out to help cover the costs related to their exercise. As an example, a gasoline tax or automobile purchase fee would go directly toward road management and creation as it does today. There are a number of categories of these user fee type taxations that are largely attributed to functions directly related. An exception are those excise taxes such as you might see on liquor or marijuana that are shared either more broadly or to related purposes.

Trying to anticipate how all these will be formally structured is a bit of a fool's errand this far out, but what we will provide is an annual listing of what taxes are being imposed, to what entities they are being returned, and also a list of projected revenues which the citizens can expect to receive benefit from such as the Great Works contemplated in the previous chapter. Our goal is complete transparency so you can see what we are doing, and part of that is our government will seek to maintain a surplus.

Let's talk about one of the historic weaknesses of republics which is their tendency to run up unsustainable amounts of debt. Canada owes about 90% of its current GDP in debt, and the United States is at 110%, with both projected to rise as entitlement requirements for older generations become manifest. All that money owed requires the payment of interest, often to foreign or international actors who require terms which we would find abhorrent to our very sense of sovereignty, and which America at least has long been able to avoid by virtue of the strength of our military. A new world where we don't spend as much on guns as the next seven countries combined will liberate our citizens and reduce our expenditures massively, but it also means we will require a new focus on saving.

As such, we very much intend to run a surplus and accept that some years of austerity may be required at the beginning of New Albion as we purge ourselves of the gluttony of the old system and lay down a foundation for the generation of real wealth, the destruction of both public and private debt from the very onset. We seek the creation of a society of production rather than wealth redistribution, whether it be through high finance and their debt bondage, and speculative interest games, or conversely, through selective welfarism through unearned support. While we will find ways to protect our most vulnerable, we define that as related to capacity instead of any supposed victim or class status.

In introducing the prohibition against wage taxes, we noted several times that income taxes are not exempt. Although this formula may evolve, it seems the fairest way to assess this is to exempt an amount equal to double the median wage to be exempted from taxation for a business owner. Such an amount could be conceivably set as low as the median income, but recognizing that people who work more deserve to keep more as a fundamentally fair assertion, we want to encourage success and that level of investment. We also note that these criteria should serve to create an upward wage pressure precisely to increase the amount the ownership class will earn, a measure we think more likely to succeed than artificial price controls on labor.

It is important to know we will not allow business owners to claim wages separate from income for businesses they possess. Should a company be owned jointly by multiple entities, for tax accounting purposes, the profit/liability shall be equal to amount of the share possessed. Expenditures will be assessed in the year of their expensing, with the capacity for owners to earn future tax credits for fixed asset investment. What this means is if a business buys infrastructure that costs a lot as a multi-year investment, we will permit them to space out the cost of that purchase over multiple years, a common business practice designed to encourage investment. But while we will allow this sort of investment, we're closing the loophole for charitable contributions.

For many years, this nonprofit deduction loophole has been used to promote the very worst ideas throughout our society, and charitable giving will now be either conducted as voluntary with no tax benefit, or with the assistance of the government. We will not permit our culture to be a clearing house in New Albion.

Without using particular numbers, the goal we have for how we elevate corporate income is to place the elevators in such a way to make it financially desirable to own a business that works in a local region and can have up to several branches, but which makes it challenging to operate entities that exist throughout the nation as a single privately held organization. There is the possibility that franchise agreements may be considered as a separate class provided ownership is decentralized, but what we are really looking to accomplish is to see our most wealthy offer the most back to society as the first goal, and more importantly, prevent the rise of economic actors who can become a monopoly in any one area. Having watched the nexus of big corporations working in connection with big government to such poor effect for the quality of life in America, New Albion is going to try a different path.

We don't want to punish success. We want to distribute it. We don't want to soak our people. We want to treat them fairly. And we want to have others pay whenever they can, which is why the Crown is authorized to both collect user fees from foreigners using New Albion services in any category, and set tariffs to protect our economy and benefit our people as we work toward self-sufficiency. America originally was funded by little more, so this is an area where we believe considerable gains can be made, and represent a source of income that will help sustain national services like our military to protect the borders as well as fund projects that will offer a material and financial return to the New Albioner folk.

There is much more to explore with how we want to structure the economy, but this gets caught up in issues of environmental integration, energy production, productive economics as opposed to speculative finance, and how we wish to redesign our lifestyle to accomplish our social goal of finding the good through our core values as repeatedly defined as our cause for being and offering service to our people. It is an ongoing conversation at the time of this writing and will be the content of the final book I plan to write of this conception quartet, where we invite your participation.

This level of detail might make it appear that we are trying to plan out the entire economy, but nothing could be further from the truth. We're trying desperately to simplify how everything works for consumer, taxpayers, and businesses alike, demolishing whole layers of bureaucracy in this process, and use the state to serve only as fair rule keeper and referee for the market. We want innovation to be rooted in and operate in service to the community, and just as we have demonstrated with our government, we're fighting for the little guy versus the big behemoth. We have a penchant for fighting for challenging causes, which honors both our settler past, and what we know we are proposing to accomplish in this hour.

New Albion is proud to offer a sensible system that gives you greater flexibility, much more transparency, and forces government to work with itself rather than against itself. Our revenue model embraces a cooperative rather than antagonistic model, allowing for local flexibility, and ensuring oversight by both legislative bodies at two levels as well as the people themselves.

Getting more and paying less is a tradition we can support.

Chapter Twelve: Military in Detail

This chapter inherently must be more speculative, but it attempts to first address the key responsibilities and divisions of authority by which we will maintain an active and vigilant self-defense, as well as the means to secure ourselves against hostile neighbors as we incorporate those areas who voluntarily seek accession into New Albion as we anticipate in our first years of existence, until the reorganization of North America is complete.

Let's start by talking about what got America into trouble. In the period between Reconstruction and the First World War, America had the world's fastest growing economy, was creating the most wealth anywhere, and expanded to fill out this continent. The state had no income tax, there was no central bank, welfare was a function of the church, and we did not have a standing army in permanent readiness to fight perpetual war.

Between 1910 and 1940, we saw each of these change where America became embroiled in two world conflicts, faced the Great Depression which the Federal Reserve was supposedly created to prevent, had socialism introduced through the New Deal, which became the foundation by which faith and family were muscled out of existence. Canada was no less the victim as Ottawa wrestled control from the provinces and the ideology of the state and university of progressive self-hatred and replacement came to proliferate. The welfare state was wedded to the warfare state, and having a large military, we became accustomed to the idea we needed to intervene everywhere, which explains America's hegemonic behavior and how the heart of the empire has a pulse now that beats to a different rhythm.

New Albion rejects that. We choose neither supremacy nor inferiority, opting for a third path of internal exploration and self-determination. Our military reflects this stance and we proudly assert publicly that the troubles of the Old World are not ones we here in the New World assume responsibility for any longer. Our ancestors came here to escape those ancient conflicts, and whether motivated by altruism or greed, the reality is the costs of being involved internationally have far exceeded the benefits, We must regroup within a land we can hold and truly embrace the idea the world is neither our plaything to exploit nor our problem to resolve. It exists, we must interact with it, but we must define ourselves internally before we can undertake such action. Our military, therefore, exists in fulfillment of this limited and clear strategic objective.

While we recognize there is a violent world out there, and think it highly likely North America will be unsettled for some time, we cannot allow these fears to cause us to overlook the reality that for some time America has served the purposes of its military much more than our armed forces have served the interests of the people. Having built such a tremendous force, we have become accustomed to its use as a universal tool to solve all our problems. This has often created hostile relations with foreign actors and overextended and entangling alliances. It has also brought us laws to fight the terrorism which we played a substantial role in creating and which have served as the very warrant by which our people now find their liberties at such peril. New Albion wants to return the primary military prowess to our citizens, not to some gargantuan bureaucracy like the Pentagon, so we deliberately have decided to avoid having a standing army save in those times where war appears imminent as identified by the Crown in concert with the Accounting.

The way we accomplish this draws upon the best practices of both the American and the Swiss traditions. Our Second Amendment right to bear arms will not be a luxury in the days ahead, but the responsibility of all able-bodied men to learn through education, and all of whom will be part of the County level militia on either active or reserve status. The size of which will be part of the determination on an annual basis, but we want all our people to have the basic skills needed to defend their home, and just as America benefits from today, we intend to have a population that is well-armed, capable and trained in using these weapons to defend their homes or repulse any invasion.

Fundamentally, this fits not only how we see the relationship between the people and the state as nationalists, but it also reflects our primarily defensive posture. We intend to be a peaceful nation by means of creation and existence, but should we be forced to conflict, anyone who messes with the Pines and Lines will be walking into a wood with several hundred million well prepared needles just waiting to strike. For our more populous neighbors who might decide at some point to try their luck at preventing our departure or in claiming our land, they would do well to think of us as friends rather than foes, because should they bring us to war, we will fight to our fullest capacity as a capable, decentralized, and ready machine to preserve our home and our safety.

I hope it does not come to that. I hope we find a mutually amicable separation that sees the huge city on the east coast choose their own path, taking Washington with them, and we will honor the chance to make lines that make sense for us both. We can depart in peace and arrange for population exchanges. But, in the end, if they decide they will not permit us to exercise liberty in our escape, I have complete confidence the loss will be much more greatly born by them, for their refusal to recognize the sovereignty of the country folk who are the very heart of New Albion. Just as America depended upon the boys of Appalachia to be their trigger finger, so too do we trust the farm boys and the hillbillies to do what they must to secure the nation.

A smaller military, especially in peace time, means massive savings, but we recognize that a permanent officer corps must be kept up to speed, and so we have provisioned for staff level officers to be available to help train militias, teach basic skills, serve as adjuncts to the higher nobility in organizational exercises to be carried out regularly. We have not yet formalized a series of ranks for the military, but the highest officers shall be known as Field Marshals for the Army and Grand Admirals for the Navy, who shall be charged with completing an equivalent series of ranks for both services. The Air Force shall be merged with the Army and the Space Force shall be merged with the Navy.

For those missions which require quicker application, the Crown is authorized to maintain a small number of units for specific and special operations deemed vital to national security and under direct command of the King. The sensitive nature of these missions requires them to remain at a high state of readiness, but in no case is this capacity to be developed to ever be larger than a division.

The other area in which permanent military deployment is authorized is as a border guard which includes serving as guards at embassies. We want to be very clear we intend to enforce our borders, and we reserve the right to deny entry to any non-citizen for any reason and we will not assume any asylum seeker has a right to show up and be admitted. Those seeking asylum in peacetime will be required to attend an embassy or follow directions as put forth by the New Albion government to gain entry. These officers will also be responsible for enforcing immigration including visa overstays. All those entering by air or land will be reviewed by the Army. Only those entering by sea or space will be reviewed by the Navy.

We also want to see the creation of a Royal Academy for the Army and for the Navy. It will be the highest honor for professionals to emerge with world class training, and we want to keep apprised of developments in international warfare, with men who serve in these positions serving also to be involved with the Crown in ensuring that New Albion maintains the ability to offer sound defense of the homeland and waters.

The Navy will operate much the same, but will keep a larger active capacity because a fleet will be maintained which is capable of protecting the homeland from external attack, deterring piracy, and defeating any force attempting to assault New Albion from the sea. This force will inherently be less capable than the American Navy, but our initial target until things settle down is parity with any other North American power with the specific ability to prevent invasion by any other global power. We will no longer assume the duty as America did of protecting global commerce, believing that should be a regional responsibility for other actors.

New Albion will have a volunteer military, especially for the Navy and the permanent Army positions, but can institute a draft during war time to bolster the military as required. Volunteers will be taken first to fill all roles required, should war be declared, and reinforcements will be provided as needed. Our goal is not to conquer any territory, but to see our homeland be made secure, so we approach conflict with this firm resolution that always seeks to secure a lasting peace as best fits the situation.

We close with consideration of what is to be likely in these coming years. Our analysis of North America which spawned the creation of our nation is there will be decades of chaos until new lines form that reflect cultural, economic, and ethnic priorities. We see the 2020's as the decade where financial neglect, military overreach, misguided immigration, and cultural insanity all combine to shock America, and Canada alongside, into permanent paralysis from which the state will not likely recover. Whether the solution offered is a totalitarian approach by the left which the changing demography suggests, or a military coup by the right, we want a third way that liberates the best places of this land from either model and New Albion is that hope.

We expect a hostile central authority, both at the national and most state levels, to try to use force to compel submission upon rural folk, people of European origin, moral leaders, and anyone who denies the authority of an increasingly totalitarian and arbitrary state. Even as I write this, we have promises from an American Governor in Virginia to go door to door to strip our people from their weapons, with nothing to be heard in protest from above as people are arming for a fight to preserve their rights. New Albion sees this as just the first herald of a decade where these actions are going to become more common and where we will see counties begin organizing far more proactively against such threats from their own elected governments. For those who live in states like Illinois or New York, the attacks will fall hardest on you, as the progressive base will angrily try to attack you using any means they can.

Against this, our survival will depend upon our ability to organize. This will be the foundation of the New Albion military, those militias which come together not to seek conquest or to steal new lands, but in defense of their very homes. We offer a framework to all those who fight tyranny, and will work to connect and develop groups all throughout this land, but especially in Appalachia, and the heartland, as the beginning of our state. We will make clear precisely how this government that lords over us is destroying its own authority through its actions, and peacefully but forcefully advance our case as a healthier and more honest alternative.

We consider ourselves a nation in exile, and as more exiles find their way to the periphery and as troubles come to our people, we will engage as our strength and resources best allow in defense and support of our people. For those who are ready to go a step further, we look to harness the critical mass to effectuate full separation. It may take only a few years, or it may require decades, depending entirely upon the public will, but these books serve as the foundation for how and why we undertake these actions.

Looking at the larger picture, it is no accident we center our homeland in Maine across northern New England, over into the Maritimes, and with an invitation to our friends in Quebec to become the seed from which all else may result. We are the periphery of empire, long neglected, but the seed of the West in North America in both French and English, and our work to develop the ideas on the ground here is already underway. The Pines and Lines flies already in Maine and New Hampshire, and what starts off with just a few will become a contagion when our southern states go blue and people realize the old world is dead.

From here, we will expand where we are requested to go, and we know this campaign to fulfill our natural borders will require us to be vigilant for a generation. We seek to defend, not destroy, and to preserve, not pre-empt. We know what we are doing is good for us up here, and for those who already know this path is right for them who are not connected to their homes elsewhere, we can always use more good people. But for those who cannot move or who love your homes precisely where you are, New Albion is an option that I think will reveal itself as far superior to what the system will permit.

Where we go from there, as ever, is up to the people, but know that our forces will work to preserve our nation, and the people who we are instructed to preserve as the key to restoring our civilization. It is a dangerous but exciting time, because we genuinely believe in New Albion. We know we have a kingdom that can stand the test of time just like the mighty woods from which we draw such inspiration and whose symbols we have adopted as our own.

From the military to the civil administration, our commitment is to uphold and promote the core four values of reason, nature, grace, and loyalty. We believe our *Atlantic Charter* reconciles the demand for order with the desire for liberty by permitting more freedoms than anywhere else on Earth with a solemn reminder to whom much is given, much must always also be expected. Our government lives these values by being honest, simple, accountable, local, and flexible, and our very best minds from the foundation moving ever forward must figure out how to employ these ideas in service of not just our people, but also our Atlantic Homeland of New Albion, the Arboreal Kingdom.

Now you know the reason why, and how we want to build our government, so be ready for the forthcoming volumes where we look at the culture and education next before concluding with energy, environment, and economics. There is a lot to figure out and discover, so we hope you join us and match your vision to ours.

Acknowledgments

New Albion grows all the time so there are always new people to thank, but I want to thank the many excellent patriots in Maine who are helping me make this a reality, and our growing friends in New Hampshire whose aid makes this project so much stronger.

I realize it is harder for our Canadian friends, but the encouragement coming from New Brunswick and les amis du Quebec sont tres precieux. We will speak for you when you cannot, and we remember we are one people whether in New England or Nouvelle France. Look for a future work in French from yours truly to introduce this concept more fully.

Special credit must be given to Kenaz Filan who has seen his name dragged through the mud for embracing reason, and whose sharp eye makes my writing so much more effective. His leadership in New Albion has been a blessing to us all.

My thanks go to you who read this, who share the ideas, and who become involved. Find us on Facebook at @atlantichomeland and check out the page to provide support at https://subscribestar.com/new-albion. If you want to find me personally, my name on Gab or Twitter is @tomkawczynski.

I want to close by thanking my wife Dana. Neither of us planned on being revolutionaries, but we also couldn't have planned on life going so insane in so many different ways. I am but a humble Regent, but she is truly a Queen amongst women for her courage, tenacity, and decency, and a blessing to us all.

I pray the Lord looks upon this enterprise with favor, for through Him, all things are truly possible. Amen.

www.ingramcontent.com/pod-product-compliance
Lightning Source LLC
Chambersburg PA
CBHW070710250726

48662CB00001B/338

9 781658 145022